STRANGE
VISIONS
HALLUCINOGEN-RELATED
DISORDERS

THE ENCYCLOPEDIA OF PSYCHOLOGICAL DISORDERS

Senior Consulting Editor Carol C. Nadelson, M.D.
Consulting Editor Claire E. Reinburg

STRANGE VISIONS

HALLUCINOGEN-RELATED DISORDERS

Linda Bayer, Ph.D.

CHELSEA HOUSE PUBLISHERS
Philadelphia

The author dedicates this book to George Marlow.
In troubled times and good ones, he has always been there for my family.
We don't know what we would have done without him in the face of evil.
Whether fighting at the Battle of the Bulge or offering wise counsel
on the home front, Marlow truly does have everything.

The ENCYCLOPEDIA OF PSYCHOLOGICAL DISORDERS provides up-to-date information on the history of, causes and effects of, and treatment and therapies for problems affecting the human mind. The titles in this series are not intended to take the place of the professional advice of a psychiatrist or mental health care professional.

Chelsea House Publishers
Editor in Chief: Stephen Reginald
Production Manager: Pamela Loos
Art Director: Sara Davis
Director of Photography: Judy L. Hasday
Managing Editor: James D. Gallagher

Staff for STRANGE VISIONS: HALLUCINOGEN-RELATED DISORDERS
Prepared by P. M. Gordon Associates, Philadelphia
Picture Researcher: P. M. Gordon Associates
Associate Art Director: Takeshi Takahashi
Cover Designer: Emiliano Begnardi

The Chelsea House World Wide Web address is
http://www.chelseahouse.com

First Printing

9 8 7 6 5 4 3 2 1

Library of Congress Cataloging-in-Publication Data

Applied for
ISBN 0-7910-5315-6

CONTENTS

PSYCHOLOGICAL DISORDERS AND THEIR EFFECT

CAROL C. NADELSON, M.D.
PRESIDENT AND CHIEF EXECUTIVE OFFICER,
The American Psychiatric Press

There are a wide range of problems that are considered psychological disorders, including mental and emotional disorders, problems related to alcohol and drug abuse, and some diseases that cause both emotional and physical symptoms. Psychological disorders often begin in early childhood, but during adolescence we see a sharp increase in the number of people affected by these disorders. It has been estimated that about 20 percent of the U.S. population will have some form of mental disorder sometime during their lifetime. Some psychological disorders appear following severe stress or trauma. Others appear to occur more often in some families and may have a genetic or inherited component. Still other disorders do not seem to be connected to any cause we can yet identify. There has been a great deal of attention paid to learning about the causes and treatments of these disorders, and exciting new research has taught us a great deal in the past few decades.

The fact that many new and successful treatments are available makes it especially important that we reject old prejudices and outmoded ideas that consider mental disorders to be untreatable. If psychological problems are identified early, it is possible to prevent serious consequences. We should not keep these problems hidden or feel shame that we or a member of our family has a mental disorder. Some people believe that something they said or did caused a mental disorder. Some people think that these disorders are "only in your head" so that you could "snap out of it" if you made the effort. This type of thinking implies that a treatment is a matter of willpower or motivation. It is a terrible burden for someone who is suffering to be blamed for his or her misery, and often people with psychological disorders are not treated compassionately. We hope that the information in this book will teach you about various mental illnesses.

The problems covered in the volumes in the ENCYCLOPEDIA OF PSYCHOLOGICAL DISORDERS were selected because they are of particular importance to young adults, because they affect them directly or because they affect family and friends. There are individual volumes on reading disorders, attention deficit and disruptive behavior disorders, and dementia—all of these are related to our abilities to learn and integrate information from the world around us. There are books on drug abuse that provide useful information about the effects of these drugs and treatments that are available for those individuals who have drug problems. Some of the books concentrate on one of the most common mental disorders, depression. Others deal with eating disorders, which are dangerous illnesses that affect a large number of young adults, especially women.

Most of the public attention paid to these disorders arises from a particular incident involving a celebrity that awakens us to our own vulnerability to psychological problems. These incidents of celebrities or public figures revealing their own psychological problems can also enable us to think about what we can do to prevent and treat these types of problems.

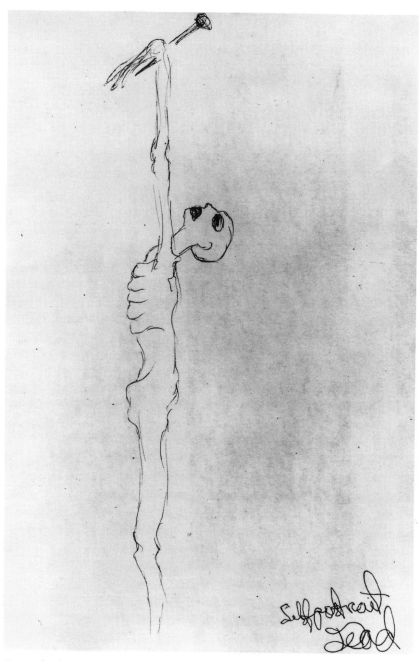

Depression is one of the most common disorders associated with the use of hallucino-
genic drugs. This drawing, made by a person under the influence of LSD, depicts a terribly
emaciated form on the verge of suicide and bears the title "Self-Portrait, Dead."

HALLUCINOGEN-RELATED DISORDERS: AN OVERVIEW

allucinogenic drugs come in a bewildering variety. Some occur in nature, such as the *mescaline* found in peyote cactus, and some are synthesized in laboratories, such as *LSD*, *PCP*, and *Ecstasy*.

These different substances are grouped under the term *hallucinogen* because they all tend to produce perceptual distortions that in some ways resemble *hallucinations* (a condition, usually involving sight, hearing, or smell, in which a person imagines that something is real when it isn't). Typical effects include visions of strange colors and shapes and an altered sense of time. Some users enjoy these perceptual alterations; however, the drugs produce dangerous side effects as well.

The physical side effects range from minor coordination difficulties to fever, coma, and even death. The psychological effects cover a similarly wide spectrum. In the short term, users may experience psychological reactions such as anxiety, depression, and delirium. In the long term the psychological repercussions can include severe mental illness. Because of the wide variety of psychological symptoms associated with the use of hallucinogens, the *Diagnostic and Statistical Manual of Mental Disorders*, published by the American Psychiatric Association, devotes an entire section to hallucinogen-related disorders.

Clearly, use of these drugs is risky. Most are also illegal. Yet their use has increased in recent years. What is it that drives people to experiment with hallucinogenic drugs?

Some hallucinogens, especially LSD, still carry a reputation they earned in the 1960s for "expanding" the mind and elevating the user to a new mental or spiritual plane. Newer hallucinogens, such as Ecstasy, have become known as "club drugs" or "party drugs," reputedly

The use of hallucinogens is on the rise, particularly among young people. To protect students from drugs of any sort, authorities have imposed harsh penalties for the distribution of drugs in or near schools. This sign warns potential dealers of the treatment they can expect if they are caught.

capable of making the user feel warm and affectionate. Accounts of such desirable effects can lead the unwary to experiment with hallucinogens.

Psychologists also believe that many of the same factors that influence other types of drug abuse prompt the use of hallucinogens: the need to escape from personal or family problems, the desire to fit in with a peer group, and so on. Thus the treatment methods for people with hallucinogen-related disorders often parallel those used for abusers of alcohol and other drugs. This treatment includes group counseling sessions, 12-step programs, and individual and family therapy.

This book offers a wide-ranging look at hallucinogens and their relationship to mental illness. Chapter 1 explores the basics of hallucinogen-related disorders, and chapter 2 traces the history of hallucinogen use from ancient times to the present. Chapters 3 through 5 examine some of the hallucinogens used most prevalently in contemporary society, while chapter 6 focuses on the reasons that people turn to such drugs. Chapter 7 concludes the book with options for getting help that are available to those involved in hallucinogen abuse.

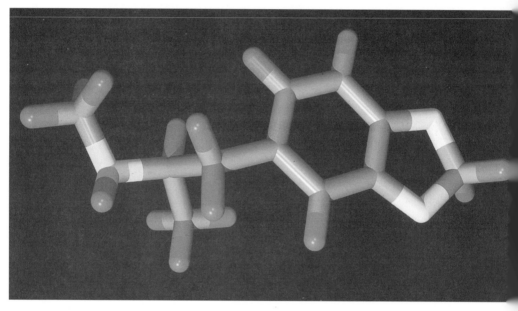

Like all molecules, drug molecules are made up of combinations of simpler elements. The molecule of the drug Ecstasy, shown here in a computer-generated model, consists of atoms of carbon, hydrogen, nitrogen, and oxygen.

1

WHAT ARE HALLUCINOGENS?

allucinogenic drugs are chemicals that alter perception, thought, and mood. Many of the common hallucinogens are known by their acronyms or their street names: LSD, PCP, and Ecstasy, for example. Most are taken orally.

The term *hallucinogenic* describes drugs that induce hallucinations—sense perceptions that don't correspond to the external world. The word *psychedelic*, which is sometimes used to describe these drugs as well, refers to their ability to change mental functioning in ways that resemble certain psychotic symptoms.

Hallucinogens can, for example, cause a person to see intensified colors and unusual shapes. A person who takes a hallucinogen may experience imagined auditory perceptions—hearing sounds that are not actually occurring. Or the person may experience bizarre sensory mixtures, including sights that are "heard" and sounds that are "tasted." Like dream states, these hallucinations seem real, and they can be either pleasurable or frightening. Altered perceptions of time and space are also common effects. Sometimes users describe out-of-body experiences, in which they seem to have transcended their physical limitations.

Most people under the influence of hallucinogens can differentiate between their drug-induced perceptions and reality. Nevertheless, symptoms produced by the drugs may become severe enough to interfere with a person's ability to function in his or her normal environment. In this case, a physician may diagnose a *hallucinogen-related disorder*.

HALLUCINOGEN-RELATED DISORDERS

The fourth edition of the *Diagnostic and Statistical Manual of Mental Disorders* (known as *DSM-IV*) identifies several types of hallucinogen-related disorders, placing them in two broad categories: hallucinogen use disorders and hallucinogen-induced disorders.

HALLUCINOGEN USE DISORDERS

Hallucinogen dependence is one type of hallucinogen use disorder. As with other types of substance dependence, its principal characteristic is a person's continued and compulsive use of the drug despite the significant problems suffered from taking it.

Problems experienced by the user may include panic attacks and loss of memory. Users may also suffer from various hangover symptoms— insomnia, fatigue, drowsiness, loss of balance, and headaches. When people with hallucinogen use disorder experience such difficulties, they are often unable to fulfill obligations at school, at work, or at home. Yet despite the disruption in their daily functioning, the users' drug-taking behavior becomes essentially compulsive. Users develop increased tolerance for the drug, requiring that they take increased amounts to attain the same effects, and they suffer severe craving when the drug is unavailable.

Hallucinogen abuse is the second type of hallucinogen use disorder. This disorder doesn't involve compulsive behavior, and the person with this diagnosis generally uses the drug less frequently than someone who is dependent on it. Nevertheless, a person in this category also suffers repeated negative effects from his or her use of the drug, such as difficulty functioning at work or at school or increased arguments with friends and family.

HALLUCINOGEN-INDUCED DISORDERS

Hallucinogen-induced disorders are conditions brought on (induced) by the use of hallucinogens. The *DSM-IV* lists a number of disorders under this heading. To illustrate the range of disorders included, we will consider three specific types.

Perhaps the simplest of the hallucinogen-induced disorders is *hallucinogen intoxication,* which refers to significant impairment in thinking or behavior that develops during or shortly after taking a hallucinogenic drug. The changes in perception, which can include *illusions* (false perceptions or false interpretations of real sensory images) and hallucinations, can be dangerous—just imagine trying to cross a busy street when your vision doesn't connect with reality. Symptoms may also include anxiety and depression; some people intoxicated with a hallucinogen have a deep fear of insanity or death.

Hallucinogen intoxication often increases the user's tendency to talk, causing the person to ramble or digress in speech and thought. Not surprisingly, hallucinogen intoxication often causes the user to have dif-

The effects of an average dose of LSD can last from 8 to 10 hours. It is not uncommon for the user to fear that he or she will never come down from this long-lasting high.

ficulty performing well at work or in social settings. Physiological signs, such as dilation of the pupils and heart palpitations, may be present as well.

Hallucinogen-induced psychotic disorder is a more severe condition. Basically, this disorder involves temporary *psychosis*—a loss of touch with reality, which can include a state of extreme *delusions* or hallucinations—that is a direct result of use of the drug. A delusion is a false belief, such as the conviction that one's thoughts can be heard by other people, that a person holds to firmly regardless of external evidence indicating otherwise. Delusions can be not only frightening but disabling as well. Moreover, people with this disorder don't perceive that the drug is producing the hallucinations. Users believe instead that what they are hearing or seeing is real. Because of the long-lasting effects of hallucinogenic drugs, the psychotic symptoms can continue as much as a month after the last use of the drug.

A third type of hallucinogen-induced disorder is called *hallucinogen persisting perception disorder* (*flashbacks*). A person suffering from this disorder has recurrences of perceptual disturbances reminiscent of those experienced during an earlier hallucinogen intoxication. Well after the drug is believed to have worn off, some or all of the hallucinogenic effects can unexpectedly return, causing considerable distress. During these flashbacks, the person may have visions of geometric forms, flares of color or intensified colors, halos around objects, and so forth. Flashbacks can be triggered by darkness, anxiety, or fatigue. They can even be self-induced, brought on when the user recalls the previous drug experience. Such episodes have been known to persist for more than five years after the hallucinogen was taken.

Other hallucinogen-induced disorders include *hallucinogen-induced mood disorder, hallucinogen-induced anxiety disorder,* and *hallucinogen intoxication delirium* (delirium is an acute state of mental confusion or disorientation).

Therapists can have difficulty diagnosing any of the hallucinogen-induced disorders when hallucinogen use is accompanied by such mental illnesses as *schizophrenia,* a psychosis for which hallucinations and other thought distortions are also symptoms. The effects of hallucinogen use may resemble or trigger a psychotic episode, or hallucinogen-related disturbances may worsen as a result of an underlying psychosis. The tangled threads of cause and effect are often difficult for a therapist to unravel.

PATTERNS OF HALLUCINOGEN USE

Use of hallucinogens generally begins in adolescence. The rate of hallucinogen drug use is about three times more common among males than among females, perhaps because the thrill seeking and risk taking involved seem more attractive to boys than to girls. Because the effects of hallucinogens are so long lasting, however, they are generally used less often than some other drugs. Even people with hallucinogen dependence may take the drug only a few times a week. Eventually users can develop a cross-tolerance among different hallucinogens: after using one hallucinogen, a person is likely to need a greater quantity of *any* hallucinogen to achieve the same feeling of intoxication. This suggests that similar chemical mechanisms are at work in the brain for all the hallucinogens.

The rate of hallucinogen use has fluctuated a great deal over the years. When hallucinogens such as LSD became popular among young people during the 1960s and 1970s, the statistics on drug prevalence reached remarkably high levels. A yearly study called the *National Household Survey on Drug Abuse* revealed that by 1979 over 25 percent of Americans between the ages of 18 and 25 had used a hallucinogen at

DRUG USE AMONG HIGH SCHOOL SENIORS

Graduating Class	Percentage
Class of 1975	16.3%
Class of 1980	15.6%
Class of 1985	12.1%
Class of 1990	9.7%
Class of 1995	13.1%
Class of 1997	15.4%
Class of 1998	14.4%

least once in their lives. Then, during the 1980s, hallucinogens gradually fell out of vogue. By the early 1990s, however, a resurgence in popularity was under way as a new generation of young people seemed unaware of the painful experiences the drugs could produce. In 1992 the *Pulse Check*—a survey measuring drug use—began to record a rise in hallucinogen availability in many areas of the country. At raves (all-night dance parties), hallucinogen use was increasingly in evidence.

The up-and-down trends in hallucinogen use since the 1970s have been tracked by the *Monitoring the Future Study*, a survey conducted annually by the Institute for Social Research at the University of Michigan. The survey measures "lifetime prevalence" of drug use among high school seniors—that is, the percentage of seniors who have ever used the drugs in question. The survey's figures for use of all types of hallucinogens are summarized in the accompanying box.

Does the slight drop-off from 1997 to 1998 herald the beginning of a new long-term trend? Researchers do not yet know for certain.

ARE WE PROGRAMMED FOR HALLUCINOGENS?

Many hallucinogens occur in nature—in plants, in fungi, and even in some animals. And, interestingly, human beings aren't the only creatures that use these substances.

Mongooses in the Hawaiian Islands and the West Indies prefer to consume the *Bufo marinus* toad, which secretes a hallucinogenic chemi-

DIAGNOSTIC CRITERIA FOR HALLUCINOGEN INTOXICATION

What does it really mean to be intoxicated with a hallucinogen? Is it the same as being drunk on alcohol? Not quite. The user is certainly impaired but in somewhat special ways.

What follows is a selection from the specific diagnostic criteria for hallucinogen intoxication given in the *Diagnostic and Statistical Manual of Mental Disorders (DSM-IV)*. The condition must meet each one of these criteria in order to be diagnosed as hallucinogen intoxication.

A. Recent use of a hallucinogen

B. Clinically significant maladaptive behavioral or psychological changes (such as marked anxiety or depression, fear of losing one's mind, impaired judgment, or impaired social or occupational functioning) that developed during, or shortly after, hallucinogen use

C. Perceptual changes occurring in a state of full wakefulness and alertness (such as subjective intensification of perceptions, illusions, hallucinations) that developed during, or shortly after, hallucinogen use

D. Two (or more) of the following signs, developing during, or shortly after, hallucinogen use:

　1. pupillary dilation

　2. tachycardia (excessively rapid heartbeat)

　3. sweating

　4. palpitations

　5. blurring of vision

　6. tremors

　7. incoordination

E. Symptoms not caused by a general medical condition and not better accounted for by another mental disorder

Hallucinogens occur in nature in the most unlikely places. The giant toad Bufo marinus, *though poisonous to dogs, possesses hallucinogenic properties that make it a favorite meal of the mongoose.*

cal, rather than toads that don't have this property. Some domesticated dogs eat hallucinogenic mushrooms, which make the canines quite playful. In the Asian forests, reindeer occasionally eat the mushroom *Amanita muscaria,* which tends to make them abnormally aggressive and loud. Various species of the cat family eat hallucinogenic plants, after which they engage in excessive sniffing, head shaking, chewing, licking, and body rolling.

In animals and in humans, hallucinogens produce their primary effects by acting on the brain. Both natural hallucinogens and synthetic varieties (those made by humans) tend to alter the production or action of *neurotransmitters,* which are chemical substances that transmit impulses between nerves. Scientists have long wondered why human beings and other animals have biological mechanisms that respond so readily to hallucinogens. After all, hallucinogens make us lose touch with reality, an effect that is presumably a hindrance to our survival. An early human trying to gather food while hallucinating would be likely to starve.

However, for humans at least, various aspects of the imagination—from dreaming to creative thinking—may involve chemicals in the body that are similar to hallucinogens. Perhaps the same sites in the brain that respond to hallucinogenic drugs also help people invent stories, compose music, create paintings, and devise new mathematical formulas. Further research is needed before we can understand these functions of the brain. But one thing is clear: we are programmed from birth to respond to hallucinogenic substances.

A South American shaman, or priest, from the Inga tribe of Colombia prepares a drink called yage (pronounced ya-hey), a tea brewed from a jungle vine. Today traditional medicine men often perform their rituals in urban areas, where artists, intellectuals, and professionals use the tea for its healing properties as well as its hallucinogenic effects.

2

HISTORY OF HALLUCINOGENS

People have known for thousands of years that hallucinogens occur naturally in certain plants and fungi. Since the late 1800s many of these substances have become available in even more potent form—their hallucinogenic elements isolated and purified. In recent decades, too, scientists have created a host of new, synthetic hallucinogens. This chapter examines several examples of naturally occurring and synthetic drugs and the social reaction to their increasing availability.

NATURALLY OCCURRING HALLUCINOGENS

In many ancient cultures, people used hallucinogenic plants for religious rituals and other purposes. Evidence of such use has been discovered on every continent and throughout the ages, from ancient Greece to India to the New World. In ancient Mexico, for instance, a hallucinogenic drug called *ololiuqui,* which is found in some types of morning glory seeds, was used in religious rites. Researchers have discovered that the drug is closely related to what we now know as LSD.

A similar history can be traced for the use of kava, a mildly hallucinogenic plant found in the South Pacific. This shrub, whose formal name is *Piper methysticum,* is a close relative of the plant from which we get ordinary black pepper. Many native peoples on the island of Fiji and elsewhere in the South Pacific would crush the roots of the shrub and use them in a mildly intoxicating beverage also known as *kava* or as *kava kava.*

Served as part of a peace ritual, *kava kava* produced various effects; it would promote relaxation, relieve pain, numb the mouth, induce sleep, and produce visions. Swedish botanist Daniel Carl Solander and artist Sydney Parkinson, who accompanied Captain James Cook on his first voyage to the South Pacific in 1768, were among the first Europeans to observe the *kava kava* ceremony, which is still practiced in some villages today.

Throughout the Amazon River basin, native shamans prepare ayahuasca *from the root of a plant. The result is a powerful hallucinogen that is used medicinally.*

Kava was also grown in New Guinea, where it was used to brew an inebriating beverage called *keu.* The plant was also found in the Solomon Islands, Samoa, Hawaii, the Philippines, and Tahiti, although it no longer grows in some of these areas today. Though kava is rare in the United States, it is not illegal, and it is sold in some beverage and health food stores.

Another traditional hallucinogen still in use today is *hoasca,* or *ayahuasca,* a potent drink made from a collection of hallucinogenic plants. Known by many other names as well (including *caapi, yagé,*

ILLUSIONS VERSUS HALLUCINATIONS

Technically, according to many specialists, the term *hallucinogenic* is misleading because the drugs in this category don't usually produce true hallucinations. Rather, they produce illusions. What is the difference? Let's look at how the *DSM-IV* defines the two terms.

In a true *hallucination,* the person perceives something that has absolutely no basis in reality—in other words, there is nothing of the sort actually stimulating the sensory organs. In an *illusion,* on the other hand, there is some kind of external stimulus, but the person misperceives or misinterprets it. In *Treatments of Psychiatric Disorders,* Thomas Ungerleider and his coauthors offer a useful example: "To 'see' someone's face melting is an illusion; to 'see' a melting face when no one is present is a hallucination."

In this sense, it is true that hallucinogenic drugs generally cause illusions rather than full-blown hallucinations. Moreover, in most cases of hallucinogen use, the user realizes that the drug is altering his or her perception of reality. Still, as illustrated throughout this book, the perceptual distortions caused by these drugs can be severe, terrifying, and psychologically disabling.

If you see the face of someone in the room with you begin to melt, that's an illusion. If you see a melting face when no one else is around, that's a hallucination. Most drugs called hallucinogens cause illusions, which are defined as the misperception of an actual stimulus.

dapa, daime, and *vegetal),* *hoasca* has long been brewed in the Amazon basin of Brazil, where it was thought to have magical properties and to connect the user with the souls of the dead. Anthropologists have reported people having *hoasca*-induced visions of jaguars, snakes, or distant cities. Some contemporary Brazilian religious movements use the brew as a sacrament.

There are simply too many naturally occurring hallucinogens found throughout the world to discuss them all here. The following sections examine those that have been especially important in North America.

PEYOTE AND MESCALINE

In North America, one of the more common hallucinogenic plants is peyote, a type of cactus that grows wild in Mexico and in the states of California, Texas, and Arizona. Peyote contains a hallucinogenic compound called mescaline.

For centuries, the Aztecs, who lived in what is now central Mexico, used this substance in religious rituals, and by the late 19th century the practice had spread to tribes in what is now the southwestern United

"Peyote buttons," the dried caps of the peyote cactus, are the source of the drug mescaline.

Frank Dayish, president of the Native American Church of North America, stands inside his church building in New Mexico. Members of the church use peyote in their religious services, and in 1997 the U.S. Department of Defense began allowing Native American soldiers on active duty to use peyote during such ceremonies.

States. Even today the Native American Church (a Christian group) employs peyote in religious ceremonies with permission from the U.S. government. Mescaline is usually taken by swallowing the dried "button" of the peyote cactus, but the drug is sometimes used in powder form. Except for religious purposes, however, peyote is now banned by the U.S. Drug Enforcement Administration.

Mescaline use usually produces kaleidoscope-like visions, along with nausea and vomiting. The substance is an *alkaloid*, a type of nitrogen compound found in many plants. Alkaloids are basic (the opposite of acidic), and many of them are pharmacologically active, which means that they act like drugs. Other common alkaloids are caffeine (found in tea leaves and coffee beans), nicotine (found in tobacco), and codeine (found in opium poppies).

Mescaline was first extracted from peyote by the German toxicologist Lewis Lewin, who discovered the plant while traveling in North America in 1886. Lewin performed various experiments with mescaline, even taking the drug himself. In a book called *Phantastica*, published in 1924, Lewin wrote that to people under the influence of this intoxicant "ordinary objects appear as marvels." He went on to speak of visions of "color-symphonies," delicate "arabesques," "radiant tapestries," and "fabulous creatures."

PSILOCYBIN

Another naturally occurring hallucinogen, *psilocybin,* is found in mushrooms of the *Psilocybe* genus. Some 15 species of this fungus grow wild in North America.

For many centuries, various societies used psilocybin mushrooms for religious rites and ceremonial observances. Ancient peoples believed that through these mushrooms the spirits sent messages to mortals.

PSYLOCYBIN: ONE USER'S EXPERIENCE

In the book *Drugs and Phantasy,* J. C. Pollard records the experiences of one female college student who took psilocybin during a scientific experiment in the 1960s. The following is an extract of her words while under the influence of the drug:

When I close my eyes, then I have all these funny sensations. Funny pictures, they're all in beautiful colors. Greens and reds and browns and they all look like Picasso's pictures. Doors opening up at triangular angles and there are all these colors . . . an unreal world. . . .

I have the feeling that someone is sticking their high-heeled shoe into the cotton in my right hand. But I can't feel it, it's not there. When I move my hand, my hands are very wet. And the lower part of my body, body, well, my body's bent. . . . Ohh. I'm moving. I look like I'm just moving. . . . Now I can see a fire. It looks like a key. . . . There's a cage and someone is opening the door of the cage. And there's a spider inside.

Mushroom stone carvings dating back to 1000 B.C. have been discovered in Central America. The earliest records of psilocybin use date to 1502, during the coronation feast of the Aztec ruler Montezuma. The Aztecs termed the mushrooms *teonanactl,* "flesh of the gods."

Scientists synthesized psilocybin in the 1950s, and researchers began investigating its properties soon after. They found that psilocybin itself isn't responsible for the hallucinogenic effects. Rather, a related compound, psilocin, is the substance that acts directly on the brain. The mushrooms contain both psilocin and psilocybin, and the body converts the latter into the former, so the mushrooms pack a double punch of psilocin. The user may experience a feeling of relaxation along with some of the perceptual distortions common to the symptoms caused by other hallucinogens. Nausea, numbness, chills, and sweating may also result. Some users undergo severe mood swings and sudden attacks of anxiety.

Today, purified psilocybin is sometimes distributed as a white powder. In addition, the psilocybin mushrooms, known as "shrooms" or "magic mushrooms," are grown in many places for personal use or for sale. Cultivation kits can be obtained by mail order, even though possession of the mushrooms is illegal in most of the United States. The use of these mushrooms can present one other serious problem: eating the wrong mushroom by mistake can prove very dangerous, since many mushrooms are highly poisonous.

ERGOT: THE SOURCE OF WITCHCRAFT?

In recent years historians have recognized that some episodes of seemingly strange behavior by large groups of people may be related to the accidental use of naturally occurring hallucinogens. The notorious witch trials that took place in Salem, Massachusetts, in 1692 are one example. After a group of young girls accused other townspeople of consorting with the devil, the number of accusations escalated, until 300 men and women were accused and 20 were executed. The mass hysteria that swept the Salem community has long fascinated historians and the general public alike. The 1996 movie *The Crucible,* based on Arthur Miller's play of the same title, presents a fictionalized version of the story.

Recent research into Salem history suggests that a kind of hallucinogenic poisoning may have been partly responsible for the witchcraft frenzy. Rye was a major crop for the Salem farmers. That year had been

The Salem Witch Trials of 1692 began after a group of young girls reported seeing townspeople consorting with the devil. Some contemporary historians believe that the visions were brought on by ergot, a hallucinogenic fungus that attacks rye.

unusually rainy in Salem, and, when rye becomes damp, the grain can develop a fungus called ergot, which is the basic source of lysergic acid—the substance used in producing the synthetic hallucinogen LSD. Thus some historians speculate that LSD-like effects may have produced the visions experienced by the young girls. Indeed, elevation maps of Salem show that the houses where the girls had their visions were concentrated in low-lying areas, where the ergot was most likely to have tainted the food and even the water supply.

OTHER DRUGS FOUND IN NATURE

Marijuana and hashish—two drugs derived from the hemp plant— are often linked in the public mind with hallucinogens, but they don't strictly belong to this category of drugs because they only infrequently produce hallucinations. Cocaine and crack, made from the coca plant, are classified as stimulants. Heroin, which comes from the poppy plant, is classified as an opiate analgesic. Other volumes in the ENCYCLOPEDIA OF PSYCHOLOGICAL DISORDERS are devoted to the psychological effects of these drugs.

SYNTHETIC HALLUCINOGENS

The best-known and most powerful synthetic hallucinogen, lysergic acid diethylamide—LSD, for short—was first synthesized in Switzerland in 1938. Albert Hofmann, a chemist working for Sandoz Laboratories, created the drug as a circulatory or respiratory stimulant. However, no benefits for the drug could be found, so its study was temporarily discontinued.

In the 1940s, interest in the drug revived. Psychiatric researchers were beginning to investigate how chemical activities in the brain correspond to certain mental states. The field of psychopharmacology—the study of the effect of drugs on the mind and behavior—was being born. Some

During the 1950s, the CIA administered LSD to unknowing subjects in order to examine the effects of the drug. This unethical and dangerous experiment was supervised by Sydney Gottlieb (left), shown here with his lawyer.

researchers became fascinated with LSD because it created symptoms that resembled those of schizophrenia and other mental illnesses. Experimenting with LSD, they thought, would give them insights into the origins and possible treatment of various mental disorders.

The term *hallucinogens* was first used in 1954 by Abram Hoffer (coauthor of the book *The Hallucinogens*) and his colleagues, who noted that these drugs "reproduce, in normal subjects, some symptoms of schizophrenia or similar psychoses." In addition to being intrigued by the research potential, some professionals thought that use of hallucinogens could directly aid certain psychiatric patients. Researchers believed that the patients' psychoses might be cured by using a combination of LSD treatment, hypnosis, and classical Freudian techniques.

During a 15-year period that began in 1950, more than a thousand scientific papers and several dozen books were written about LSD. Six international conferences were devoted to the topic. Marketed as a psychiatric cure-all, LSD was prescribed for more than 40,000 patients. However, very little medical good came from all this activity.

Eventually Paul H. Hoch (coeditor of *Psychopathology of Schizophrenia*) and his coworkers in New York City proved that LSD and mescaline actually aggravated the symptoms of psychotic patients. Experiments conducted at the Addiction Research Center in Lexington, Kentucky, demonstrated that people who took LSD and similar drugs developed a tolerance to them, so that over time they needed to consume increasing amounts of the drug to produce the same high. Thus, LSD didn't appear to cure anything. Ironically, however, researchers learned that some of the drugs that neutralized hallucinogens proved to be useful in treating schizophrenia as well.

THE PSYCHEDELIC SUBCULTURE

Along with their appeal to researchers and therapists, LSD and other hallucinogens began to gain a wider following among the public in the 1950s. In *The Doors of Perception,* a 1954 book often credited with stimulating popular interest in hallucinogens, the famous British author Aldous Huxley claimed that these drugs cleansed a person and allowed the world to be encountered anew, "as Adam may have seen it on the day of creation."

By the mid-1960s the interest had grown into a widespread mystique, especially among young people in the United States. The term *psychedelic,* suggested in 1957 by Humphry Osmond (coeditor of the book

Timothy Leary experimented with LSD in the 1960s and advocated its use as a shortcut to spiritual growth. By the 1990s, he had given up on the drug and turned to designing hallucination-like effects by computer. Leary died of cancer in 1996.

Psychedelics and coauthor of *The Hallucinogens*), became the general descriptive label for LSD and other hallucinogenic drugs that were believed to open the user's mind to a deeper sense of reality. Timothy Leary, a professor at Harvard University, thought LSD was a mystical drug that could bring salvation. Leary went on a virtual crusade to convert academics, entertainers, medical personnel, philosophers, scientists, and religious thinkers to this belief in the drug's ability to provide an instant path to enlightenment.

The use of psychedelic drugs, along with marijuana and hashish, formed part of the counterculture that had evolved by the late 1960s. Protest music, antiwar sentiments, long hair, permissive sexual behavior, a rejection of U.S. materialism, and the use of mind-altering drugs all combined to set young people apart from the society of their elders.

Jerry Garcia, lead guitarist for the Grateful Dead, set an example of drug abuse for two generations of his fans. The abuse of drugs caused him to grow old before his time. Prior to his death in 1995—at age 53—he was quoted as saying, "I'm sick of being a junkie."

Psychedelic drugs were plentiful at many rock concerts, and popular songs, such as the Beatles' "Lucy in the Sky with Diamonds," contained hidden (or not-so-hidden) references to drugs. The music played by such counterculture bands as the Grateful Dead became known as acid rock—"acid" being a nickname for LSD.

Some of the results of the infatuation with LSD were tragic. Terrifying "bad trips" could last as long as 12 hours (see the section "Bad Trips" in chapter 3 for further information). Some users leaped to their deaths from the roofs of buildings in the mistaken belief that they could fly. Cruel experiments in which LSD was given to unsuspecting prison inmates and mental patients led to gruesome experiences for the victims. Frightening flashbacks often recurred days, weeks, or even months after use of the drug. All in all, the high hopes that some people had held for LSD's ability to produce positive effects were eventually dashed, and those who survived having taken the drug were left to suffer the disastrous consequences.

LEGISLATION AGAINST HALLUCINOGENS

In May 1966, in response to growing anxiety about the use of hallucinogens, Congress passed a measure known as the Drug Abuse Control Amendment, which banned the public use and sale of peyote, mescaline, LSD, and several other drugs. Pharmaceutical companies had to stop manufacturing these substances and turn over their supplies to the National Institute of Mental Health. Then in 1970 the Controlled Substances Act instituted a ranking system placing drugs on a scale from Schedule I to Schedule V, with each rise in level representing drugs with an increased degree of medical usefulness and a decreased risk for abuse.

Since that time, LSD and other hallucinogens have had an official place in the ongoing public health effort aimed at discouraging illicit drug use (see Appendix: U.S. Drug Schedules). The struggle has been difficult, however; when one drug wanes in popularity, another takes its place.

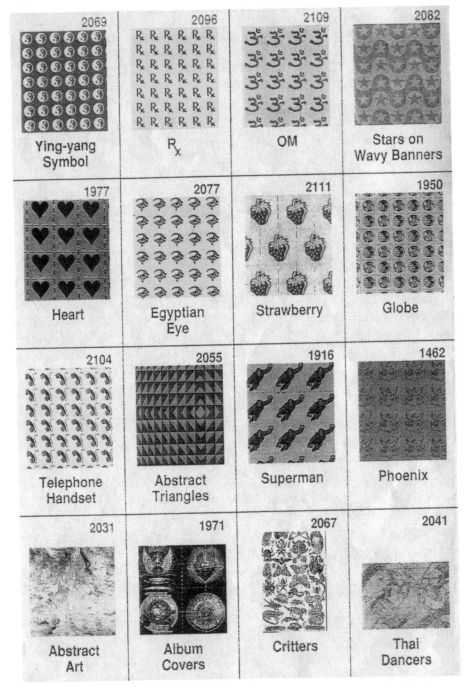

2069	2096	2109	2082
Ying-yang Symbol	R_x	OM	Stars on Wavy Banners
1977	2077	2111	1950
Heart	Egyptian Eye	Strawberry	Globe
2104	2055	1916	1462
Telephone Handset	Abstract Triangles	Superman	Phoenix
2031	1971	2067	2041
Abstract Art	Album Covers	Critters	Thai Dancers

LSD is such a concentrated drug that a single dose can be ingested from a tiny bit of blotting paper. Decorating the paper has been a kind of underground art form since the 1960s.

3

LSD

ysergic acid diethylamide (LSD) is the most potent hallucinogen known
to humanity. Dosages of LSD are measured in micrograms—millionths
of a gram—because so little is necessary to produce a powerful reaction.
By comparison, dosages of heroin and cocaine are measured in milligrams, or
thousandths of a gram. LSD produces hallucinations in humans at a dose of a
mere 25 micrograms. The drug is 100 times stronger than psilocybin, which is
4,000 times more powerful than mescaline.

LSD is usually taken orally, but it can also be injected, inhaled through the
nose, or even absorbed through the skin. When it is taken by mouth, the
effects are generally felt within 30 minutes. Sometimes an hour will pass
before the drug user experiences more intense reactions. An average oral dose
of LSD is 50 to 100 micrograms, though higher and lower doses are sometimes
used. Psychological, perceptual, and behavioral effects of the drug persist from
8 to 12 hours and wear off gradually.

Researchers believe that LSD produces its effects by stimulating certain
brain receptors. In the brain a nerve cell that is sending a signal releases one or
more chemical neurotransmitters; the special receptors on an adjacent nerve
cell react to those chemicals to receive the signal. In the case of LSD, the receptors involved are designed to respond to an important neurotransmitter called
serotonin. LSD causes some of the serotonin receptors to react as if they were
getting signals even when they aren't.

The rate of LSD use declined during the 1980s but has shown a marked
upswing in recent years. According to the *Monitoring the Future Study,* the percentage of students who used LSD in the high school class of 1998 was actually higher than that in the class of 1975: 12.6 percent versus 11.3 percent.
Those who still think of LSD as an old-fashioned "hippie" drug are unaware of
current trends.

HOW LSD IS MADE AND SOLD

Although chapter 2 classifies LSD as a synthetic hallucinogen, it may be more accurate to call it semisynthetic. The diethylamide portion is synthetic. The lysergic acid portion, however, usually comes from ergotamine tartrate, a substance derived from the ergot fungus *Claviceps purpurea*, which grows on rye and other grains, as well as on certain other types of plants. LSD can also be made from lysergic acid amide, a chemical found in morning glory seeds.

After the raw material for making LSD is acquired from sources in Mexico, Costa Rica, Europe, or Africa, it is produced in clandestine laboratories within the United States, many of them located in California. Only a small amount of ergotamine tartrate is needed to make large batches of LSD. For instance, 25 kilograms of ergotamine tartrate yield 5 or 6 kilograms of pure LSD crystal that, under ideal circumstances, can be processed into 100 million dosage units of LSD—more than enough to fill the annual U.S. demand. LSD produced in this way is relatively inexpensive and very pure.

On the street, LSD is sold in the form of tablets, capsules, or liquid. Often it is distributed as decorated blotting paper on which drops of solution have been placed. The drug has no color or odor, but it has a slightly bitter taste.

THE IMPACT OF LSD

Perceived distortions of color, size, shape, proportion, and distance are common effects of LSD use. Sometimes objects appear to change shape and color or seem to metamorphose into different objects. People may seem unfamiliar to the LSD user. *Synesthesia*, or mixing of senses—the impression that colors can be smelled or heard, for example—is also common.

People who have taken LSD may find that their sense of time is affected as well. Minutes may seem like hours. The user's mind may seem to be racing while everything appears to be moving at a snail's pace.

Sometimes LSD users describe feeling a great sense of spiritual insight or oneness with the world. The boundary between the user's body and the environment may seem to dissolve. It is this feeling that gave the drug its mystical appeal to the counterculture. This sense of deeper comprehension generally fades, however, even before the drug's other effects do. A young woman named Clair Brush described this sort of temporary revelation to Tom Wolfe, whose 1968 book *The Electric Kool-Aid Acid Test* detailed countercultural experiments with LSD. After she had consumed some LSD-laced Kool-Aid, said Brush, "a great flash of insight came to me. I've forgotten it now, but there was one instant when everything fell into place and made sense, and I said aloud, 'Oh, of course!'"

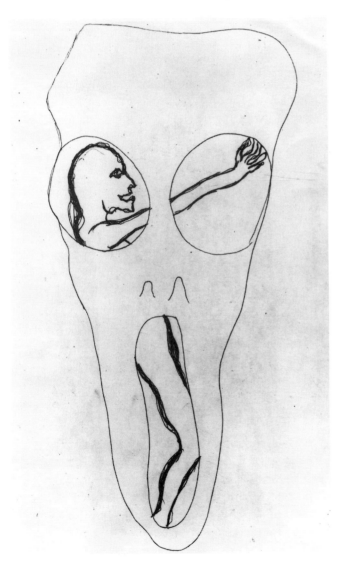

A drawing created during an LSD trip shows one person trapped inside the face of another. Users of the drug experience distorted perceptions: objects may change shape or combine in strange ways.

Another common psychological effect of LSD—as the authors of the chapter "The Hallucinogens and Cannabis" in *Treatments of Psychiatric Disorders*, report—is depersonalization, in which the person feels detached from him- or herself. An LSD user may feel as though he or she has separated into two people—the first person is having the drug experience while the second is observing. Sometimes the LSD user cannot distinguish where his or her own body stops and the external environment begins.

Dramatic mood swings frequently occur. Euphoria—a sense of extreme elation—may be replaced by severe depression. The person may laugh or cry for no apparent reason.

Derealization, or a dreamlike state in which nothing seems real, may also occur. The user may not know if he or she is awake or asleep. People who take LSD may have difficulty distinguishing between present, past, and future.

Judgment deteriorates, as do motor skills, intellect, reason, and concentration. People on LSD can be a danger to themselves or others because they cannot always recognize threatening situations posed by heights, sharp objects, weapons, or motor vehicles.

Somatic (bodily) reactions to LSD include dizziness, blurred vision, tremors, and numbness and tingling. LSD causes the pupils of the eye to dilate; it tends to increase heart rate, blood pressure, body temperature, and blood sugar.

"BAD TRIPS"

An unpleasant experience from taking LSD is as likely to occur as a good one. The impact of the drug is extremely unpredictable. Its effects are influenced by a number of factors, including the people with whom the user takes the drug, the conditions under which the drug is taken, the personality of the user, and the quality and quantity of the LSD consumed.

A "bad trip" characteristically results in a panicky feeling of loss of control and the desire for the experience to end. The user may become frantic after realizing that he or she has boarded an emotional roller coaster that will endure for hours. Sometimes a terrified LSD user can be "talked down" or returned to a feeling of calm by a friend or health care professional who takes the individual to a safe, quiet place and offers reassurance and distraction. A person who has taken LSD should

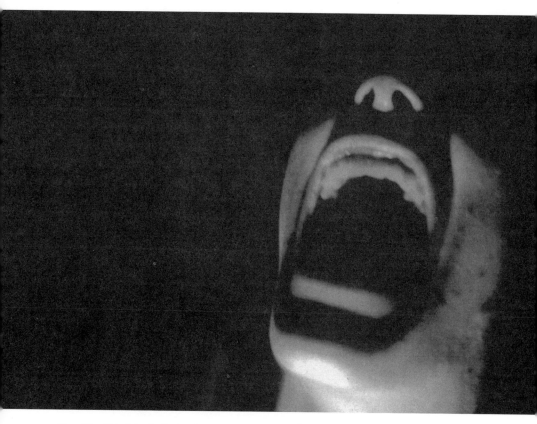

On a "bad trip," the hallucinations can get scary. Feelings of panic, fear, and loss of control may lead to a desperate attempt at suicide.

not be left alone or allowed to drive a car. "Bad trips" have caused users to attempt suicide or otherwise endanger their lives.

FLASHBACKS

Flashbacks (described in chapter 1 as the recurrence of symptoms of the LSD trip that can happen days, weeks, months, or even years after the drug is taken) have plagued many LSD users. Flashbacks tend to be negative experiences, with the loss of control over one's body and mind becoming very frightening. The daughter of television personality Art Linkletter killed herself in 1970 during a flashback that occurred six months after she had taken LSD.

Flashbacks can happen after just one experience with LSD, but they occur more commonly among chronic LSD users. A flashback may start

The use of LSD during pregnancy increases the risk of miscarriage, stillbirth, or spontaneous abortion. Birth defects to her child remain a danger even years after a woman has stopped using the drug.

just as a person is falling asleep, while he or she is driving a motor vehicle, or at times of stress. Use of any other psychoactive drug, including alcohol, can precipitate a flashback.

PARANOID AND SCHIZOID REACTIONS

LSD is sometimes called a *psychotomimetic* drug because it can mimic such states as *paranoia,* which is a symptom of schizophrenia and other psychotic disorders. A paranoid person is unduly fearful that others are trying to hurt him or her. LSD can produce a similar reaction, causing users to feel persecuted.

During LSD-induced psychotic episodes, a person's sense of identity can break down. In such a schizoid state, a user may be plagued by an inferiority complex and conclude that his or her life is worthless. Or the person may experience delusions of grandeur, imagining that he or she is superhuman, immune from all forms of injury. LSD users may believe that they can fly or that God will protect them from all sources of harm.

Especially in those who are already susceptible to psychosis, LSD use can trigger a full-blown psychotic event. And sometimes the schizoid state (which is characterized by social withdrawal and restricted emotional expression) or the paranoid state doesn't subside when drug use stops.

ADDITIONAL PROBLEMS CONNECTED WITH LSD

Using LSD can lead to many other psychological disorders. As already mentioned, the dramatic mood swings caused by LSD can lead to severe depression. When severe enough, LSD-induced depression can lead to suicide. A manic reaction, in which the person becomes overly excited and hyperactive, may occur as well. Manic symptoms may also include endless talking and a sense of unlimited exuberance.

LSD use can also prompt development of a catatonic state, in which a person will sit, lie, or stand unmoving for hours at a time. On occasion, too, the drug can cause the user to develop convulsions, during which the victim shakes uncontrollably. The user may fall down, writhing on the floor, eyes rolling back and tongue blocking the windpipe. Anyone experiencing such a convulsion needs immediate medical attention.

When people have taken LSD frequently for a number of years, their electroencephalograms, which indicate brain-wave patterns, often appear abnormal. It is possible that these abnormal patterns would have appeared without drug use or that they contributed to the person's

THE "JOAN OF ARC" OF LSD

Albert Hofmann, an early LSD researcher who is sometimes called the father of the drug, generally believed in its mystical benefits, but he was also aware of its dangers. In his book *LSD: My Problem Child,* he told the story of a young American woman who had visited him at his laboratory in Switzerland.

When she knocked at the door of his private office without warning, introducing herself as Joan from New York, he asked how she had maneuvered past the security checks. "I am an angel," she told him; "I can pass everywhere." It turned out that she had been taking LSD, and she had been inspired with the idea for a great mission. To rescue the United States from its many difficulties (including, at that time, the Vietnam War), she planned to reorient the president's thinking by having him take LSD. For this incredible project, she wanted Hofmann's help. Her name, she thought, would help convince people that she was the Joan of Arc of the United States.

With difficulty, Hofmann tried to explain to her that the scheme wouldn't work. She left his office disappointed but phoned the next day to ask for help because she was out of money. Hofmann took her to a friend, who found her a job and a place to stay. Within a few weeks, Joan vanished from Switzerland. Some months later, Hofmann learned that she was in a psychiatric hospital in Israel. Her story, he admitted in his book, stood out in his mind as "an example of the tragic effects of LSD."

drug-taking behavior. Nevertheless, many physicians are concerned that LSD use may cause irreversible changes in the brain.

Women who use LSD during pregnancy increase their risk of having a miscarriage or stillbirth. An unusually high number of spontaneous abortions occur among pregnant women who take LSD. Researchers don't yet know exactly why, but there is speculation that the drug may alter fetal blood flow, uterine contractions, or other bodily systems. And if the pregnancy of a woman who uses LSD reaches full term, there is an increased risk her child will have birth defects.

Finally, like chronic marijuana users, people who take LSD repeatedly may suffer from amotivational syndrome—that is, they lose their motivation to do ordinary activities. They may show little interest in school, work, friends, or family. Essentially, the unmotivated individual becomes dysfunctional and has little desire to do anything except take drugs. The cause and effect in such cases is debatable. Which comes first, the drug use or the lack of motivation for other activities? Each may affect the other.

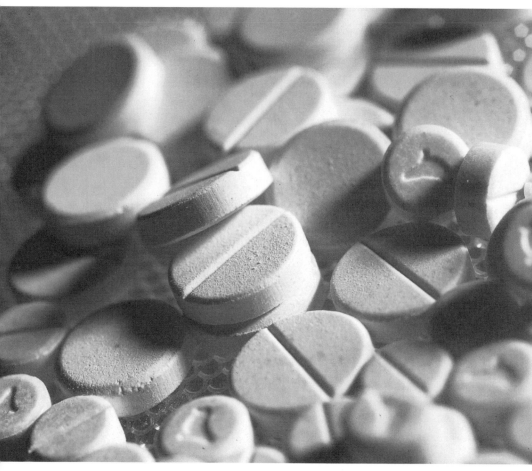

PCP was developed in the 1950s as an intravenous anesthetic. Its medicinal use was discontinued in the mid-1960s, but it then turned up in San Francisco and New York City as a street drug. In its relatively inexpensive pill form, it was used as a substitute for cocaine, mescaline, or psychedelic mushrooms.

4

PCP

Phencyclidine is an entirely synthetic substance that is relatively easy to manufacture. It is commonly known by the acronym PCP, which is derived from the drug's chemical name: 1-(1-*phenylcyclohexyl*)-*piperidine*. In the 1960s the drug's street name was the "*peace pill*."

Because PCP's effects tend to differ somewhat from those of such drugs as LSD and Ecstasy (which is discussed in chapter 5), the *DSM-IV* devotes a special section to "phencyclidine-related disorders." Other authorities, such as the Substance Abuse and Mental Health Services Administration and the National Institute on Drug Abuse, tend to group PCP with the hallucinogens.

The drug was commercially developed by Parke, Davis and Company in the late 1950s for use as an intravenous anesthetic. Until 1965 it was used in hospitals for surgical patients and burn victims. By then, however, adverse side-effects were being reported.

After surgery, many patients who had been given phencyclidine experienced confusion, terror, and unpleasant hallucinations. These negative psychoactive properties of PCP proved so severe that medical use in humans was halted in 1965. Today the drug is carefully regulated by the government for distribution to licensed researchers. The federal government itself manufactures the drug, and all other production is illegal.

However, as a street drug—sold under names like "angel dust" and "crystal"—PCP has proved hard to control. It first appeared on the streets of San Francisco in the 1960s and shortly thereafter in Greenwich Village, New York. Users frequently reported unpleasant reactions, but because the pill was inexpensive, it was frequently substituted for cocaine, psychedelic mushrooms, and mescaline. By the late 1960s the drug's bad reputation caused its temporary disappearance. In 1972, however, it reappeared as a liquid or powder that could be added to mint, parsley, oregano, tea, tobacco, or marijuana and then smoked.

Like LSD, PCP has waxed and waned in popularity. The Drug Abuse Warning Network (DAWN) reported that between 1972 and 1975 PCP moved from 23rd to 5th place on the scale of abused drugs. By 1981, it had dropped back to 10th place. In the *Monitoring the Future* study of high school seniors, 12.8 percent of students in the class of 1979 reported that they had used PCP at some time in their lives. In the 1990s, however, the corresponding figure didn't exceed 4 percent.

PCP AND ITS RELATIVES

In its pure form, PCP is a white crystalline powder that dissolves in water or alcohol. It has a distinctively bitter taste. Because it often contains contaminants, it may appear tan or brown and may be gummy in texture. It is sometimes dyed different colors. Some dealers have been known to add formaldehyde or roach spray to the preparation, giving it a chemical odor. Because PCP is frequently substituted for other drugs, people sometimes do not know they have taken PCP.

The drug can be taken orally, intravenously, by smoking, or by "snorting" through the nostrils. People who take PCP are often poly-

In pure form, PCP is a white crystalline powder. When it reaches the street, however, it is almost never pure and may be brown in color with a gummy texture.

drug users—given to taking other drugs as well, either simultaneously or separately. PCP can be sold as powder or pills, but most recently it is often sprayed on thin marijuana cigarettes; the resulting combination is often referred to as "loveboat." Marijuana laced with PCP is also called a "killer joint" or "crystal supergrass."

To complicate the situation, there are at least 30 PCP analogs (drugs with similar chemical structures and properties). By slightly altering the molecular structure of an existing drug, black-market chemists can create a new drug, or analog, that is technically legal because it has not yet been tested. In this way, they are able to bypass the U.S. Drug Schedules instituted by the 1970 Controlled Substances Act. Amateur chemists working in illegal labs often create PCP analogs and pass them off as PCP. Some of these substances have poisonous by-products that can be lethal to users. For example, PCC (formally known as 1-piperidinocyclohexane carbonitrile) is a PCP analog that can produce cyanide in the user's blood. Symptoms such as bloody vomiting, diarrhea, and abdominal cramps occur after PCC ingestion. *Ketamine*, another dangerous PCP analog, is discussed in chapter 5.

In chemical terms, the actions of PCP and its relatives on the body are complicated. They affect many different neurotransmitters in the brain, including glutamate and dopamine. For this reason, their physical and psychological effects are quite variable and unpredictable.

THE EFFECTS OF PCP

One of the effects of PCP—and the main reason for its appeal—is a frequent sense of stimulation and even euphoria that results from taking the drug. Some users also report having sensations of power and strength. Generally, PCP doesn't often produce the kind of vivid, colorful visions associated with LSD and mescaline use; rather, it has a numbing effect on mind and body. Researchers describe PCP as a *dissociative anesthetic* because it allows people to be aware of physical sensations such as touch and pressure while blocking the perception of pain.

In their book *Buzzed*, Cynthia Kuhn, Scott Swartzwelder, and Wilkie Wilson have described the PCP-induced state as "similar to getting drunk, taking amphetamine, and taking a hallucinogen simultaneously." Yet reactions to PCP differ widely from person to person, depending on the user's personality, family or individual history of mental disorder, dosage, and past drug experience. The following sections describe some

In its most common method of consumption, PCP is sprayed on marijuana cigarettes and smoked, a combination known as "loveboat," "killer joint," or "crystal supergrass."

of the more notable symptoms of the drug, but it is important to keep in mind that one frightening feature of PCP is its unpredictability.

SHORT-TERM EFFECTS

PCP use often produces distortions in sight, hearing, and touch. As with alcohol, the drug typically causes an altered sense of the body. It may cause lack of coordination and dizziness. In many users PCP also results in amnesia (memory loss). Rapid vertical eye movements are another symptom of PCP use.

More than other drugs, with the possible exception of alcohol, PCP is closely associated with unpredictable, bizarre, and aggressive behavior that can lead to injury or death for both the user and others. People under the influence of PCP may experience severe anxiety and tension and may become violent and destructive. PCP often causes confusion in the user, interfering with his or her ability to have good judgment, make intelligent choices, and participate in goal-directed activities.

In severe cases, PCP can produce short-term psychoses that are virtually indistinguishable from symptoms of schizophrenia. Users may experience a full range of psychotic symptoms, including paranoia; delusions; and *catatonia*, or catatonic schizophrenia (a complete lack of attention to surroundings, usually coupled with inappropriate stiffening or loosening of the muscles but sometimes also with excessive activity and excitement). In large doses, PCP can bring on muscle rigidity, seizures, or coma (deep sleep from which a person cannot be awakened) lasting from hours to days.

LONG-TERM EFFECTS

If a habitual PCP user tries to discontinue use of the drug, severe depression may result. The depression can last from a few days to several months, and the risk of attempted suicide at such times is high. Often hospitalization is required for long-term PCP users, and antidepressant medication may be necessary.

Other common long-term symptoms include increased nervousness, paranoid delusions, violent behavior, and homicidal inclinations. Many chronic PCP users feel increased anger, irritability, and loneliness and demonstrate antisocial behavior. Other symptoms include slurred speech, aphasia (inability to recall appropriate words), impaired articulation of words, speech blockage, general memory loss, and periods of disorientation.

Not surprisingly, PCP users show a high incidence of divorce, job loss, and disruption in education. During periods of intense PCP use, they tend to eat little (often only one meal a day), causing significant weight loss. Constipation, urinary hesitancy, and uncontrollable eye movements sometimes accompany extended PCP use as well.

The National Institute on Drug Abuse considers PCP (unlike LSD) to be addictive. That is, users can develop a psychological dependence on the drug, a true craving for it, and a compulsion to obtain it. Once dependent, users may take the drug two or three times a day, making their long-term recovery especially difficult.

Prolonged PCP use can lead to severe depression and, ultimately, suicide. PCP users also exhibit nervousness, paranoia, and aggressive, violent behavior.

TREATMENT FOR PCP USE

Because PCP is highly fat soluble, much of it is stored in the body's fatty or brain tissue; only about half the PCP consumed is eliminated within three days. As a result, there is great risk of overdose and the prolonged effects that can lead to coma or PCP psychosis.

There is currently no antidote for PCP symptoms—no known substance that can reverse the effects of the drug. To flush out patients' systems, hospital staff often administer ammonium chloride tablets or cranberry juice with vitamin C. These substances help draw PCP out of the tissues and into the bloodstream, where it is eventually eliminated by the body.

Many PCP users land in emergency rooms, where, because PCP blocks the sensation of pain, they must be prevented from inadvertently hurting themselves. During the period of acute intoxication, which normally lasts six to eight hours, the patient is typically isolated in a room with minimal stimulation. Physical restraints are sometimes required. The patient may also be given a tranquilizer such as Valium (diazepam) to reduce agitation. The "talking down" approach employed for LSD users generally doesn't work for those affected by PCP; in fact, it may cause patients to become even more disturbed.

Psychosis resulting from PCP use is sometimes treated with prescription medications such as Haldol (haloperidol), often combined with a tranquilizer. Thereafter, long-term psychological therapy is usually recommended.

Because its effects include euphoria, loss of inhibition, and openness to others, Ecstasy has become a popular party drug, often making appearances at rock concerts and all-night raves.

5

ECSTASY AND OTHER DRUGS

Hallucinogens are sometimes called "club drugs" because they are used at dance clubs that cater to young people. Children as young as 13 and 14 years old sometimes attend all-night raves at which drugs can be found. Some of the most popular drugs sold and consumed at such clubs (Ecstasy [MDMA], *Nexus*, and ketamine) are discussed in this chapter.

ECSTASY (MDMA) AND MDA

Methylenedioxymethamphetamine (MDMA) is a synthetic drug that produces both psychedelic and stimulant effects. As the chemical name indicates, it is related to amphetamine, the well-known (and frequently abused) stimulant. Though first created early in the 20th century, MDMA was scarcely used clinically until some psychotherapists prescribed it for their patients in the 1980s. Its effects were too unpredictable, however, and by 1988 the U.S. Food and Drug Administration had reclassified MDMA as a substance with no approved medical use.

PATTERNS OF USE OF MDMA

As an illegal club drug, most often found in tablet or capsule form, MDMA is known as Ecstasy, X-TC, and Adam. It has been used at rock concerts, at raves, and on college campuses. Some who are aware of the dangers associated with such drugs as cocaine and heroin are ignorant of the dangers of taking MDMA.

The *Monitoring the Future* study did not begin to track MDMA use until 1996. Since then, survey data show that about 6 to 7 percent of 12th graders have used the drug at least once, with percentages nearly half as high for 8th graders, indicating that use of this drug can begin at an early age. According to estimates by the Drug Abuse Warning Network (DAWN), emergency room reports of MDMA use indicated an increase of more than 800 percent from 1993 to 1997.

NOT SO ECSTATIC: THE ECSTASY HANGOVER

In one experiment to test the effects of Ecstasy, a British researcher named Valerie Curran approached the matter head on—she set up a small laboratory inside a London club where the drug was being used. Her procedures and results were reported by David Concar in a fascinating article in *New Scientist*.

Curran persuaded two dozen of the club's patrons to volunteer for testing immediately after a Saturday evening at the club. She separated them into two groups: those who said they had used only alcohol that night and those who said they had taken Ecstasy. The first tests were conducted at once, on the premises. Then Curran did follow-up tests at the volunteers' homes the next day and again the following Wednesday.

She tested the subjects for both memory and mood. One test of "working memory" and concentration involved counting backward in sevens from a three-digit number. On Saturday and Sunday, the Ecstasy users scored almost twice as poorly on this test as the alcohol users. On Wednesday, the difference between the two groups had narrowed but was still apparent. The mood tests were even more interesting. On Sunday both groups were irritable, anxious, and depressed—hungover, in essence. By Wednesday the drinkers had escaped their hangovers, but the Ecstasy users were even more depressed than they had been three days earlier. On Wednesday, moreover, the Ecstasy users experienced twice as much anxiety as the drinkers and were also more restless and irritable.

Curran noted that there was considerable variation from one person to another. But "some of these people," she said, "would have qualified for antidepressants"—that is, prescription drugs to relieve their symptoms. Although more research is needed before we can fully understand the effects of Ecstasy and related drugs, much of the evidence already in demonstrates experiences that are far from ecstatic.

EFFECTS OF MDMA

Ecstasy use tends to cause a loss of inhibition and a sense of euphoria. Other effects include a sense of openness to other people, a deep sense of caring, and a decline in anger or aggressiveness. For these reasons, Ecstasy has been called a "feel-good drug" or a "hug drug"; it is also known as an aphrodisiac. The effects of an average-size dose may last four to six hours although they may last longer.

Unfortunately, adverse psychological reactions to MDMA are quite common. These include psychotic episodes, in which the user loses touch with reality; panic attacks, in which the user is overcome with irrational fear; and long-term sensory distortions. Severe anxiety, paranoia, and depression can persist for weeks after use of the drug.

Even short-term visual and auditory distortions caused by MDMA can last 10 to 12 hours, making driving under the influence of this drug particularly hazardous. MDMA can also cause dehydration, appetite suppression, and disruption of heartbeat. Increases in heart rate and blood pressure are particularly problematic for people with circulatory or heart disease. Other problems related to the use of Ecstasy include high temperature, muscle tension, involuntary teeth clenching, nausea, blurred vision, faintness, chills, and sweating.

BRAIN CHEMISTRY AND MDMA

Like other hallucinogens, Ecstasy achieves its effects by altering neurotransmitter systems in the brain. It increases the amount of the neurotransmitter serotonin that nerve cells release, while it also slows down the rate at which serotonin is reabsorbed into the cells. Ecstasy also affects the neurotransmitters dopamine and norepinephrine.

There is alarming evidence that Ecstasy does more than change neurotransmitter systems temporarily—it may permanently damage the actual nerve cells in the brain. The spate of recent research on the drug has been reviewed in journals, in books, and in a *New York Times* article by Sandra Blakeslee. The research indicates that Ecstasy may literally crop off parts of the nerve cells that release neurotransmitters. Although the parts may grow back, the new growths are abnormal.

Most of the studies on Ecstasy have been performed on animals, and more research is needed to confirm results; however, findings indicate that people who take high doses of the drug may suffer permanent brain damage. This, in turn, may lead to problems such as chronic sleep, memory, and mood disorders. The degree of damage is probably related to the amount of the drug used and the frequency with which it is taken.

MDA

Methylenedioxyamphetamine (MDA), the parent drug (or source drug) and an analog of MDMA, is another amphetamine-like substance that has been abused. Similar in chemical structure to Ecstasy, MDA

Ecstasy laboratories imprint their pills with logos to distinguish their products. The logos are designed to appeal to young customers.

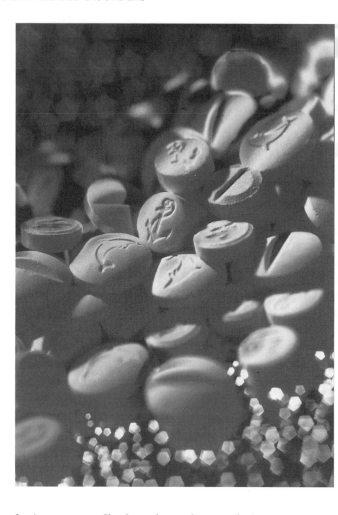

affects serotonin-producing nerve cells that play a direct role in regulating aggression, sleep, sexual activity, mood, and sensitivity to pain. This action is probably what gives MDA its purported ability to produce heightened sexual feelings, a sense of tranquillity, and sociability. As with Ecstasy, the brain damage may be permanent.

NEXUS

Nexus, also called 2-CB or Erox, is a relatively new substance. The official name of this synthetic analog is 4-bromo-2,5-dimethoxyphene-thylamine. Other street names for the drug are Bromo, Spectrum, and XTC (which is often confused with Ecstasy). Nexus is related to MDMA and MDA as well as to mescaline.

PATTERNS OF USE

Nexus usually comes in the form of red pills or white powder. Although Nexus is sometimes distributed at parties, its hallucinogenic effects have prompted some people to use it at home or in other quiet settings where there is less visual stimulation. Sometimes Nexus is consumed in combination with MDMA.

EFFECTS OF NEXUS

The effects of Nexus last from three to six hours. At a low dosage (5 to 10 milligrams), the drug has mild stimulating effects. At a higher dosage, Nexus produces marked visual hallucinations with intense colors and patterns. The user's other perceptual and sensory systems also are affected. In contrast to MDMA, which may reduce male potency, Nexus seems to have sexually enhancing properties for both men and women and is sometimes sold as an aphrodisiac.

Sensitivity to Nexus varies greatly from person to person, though reactions at relatively low doses have been reported in all people. The psychedelic reactions from taking high doses can be terrifying, particularly for inexperienced users. When the substance is sold as XTC, it is often confused with the drug Ecstasy; in this case, uncertainty about the dosage of the drug received may result. Those using Nexus regularly more than once a week can develop a tolerance to the drug that requires them to take increased amounts to obtain the same experience. Yet the difference in size between a dose that produces pleasant hallucinations and one that results in a "bad trip" is quite small.

Temporary psychosis caused by taking Nexus has been reported— that is, users may lose touch with reality. Acute panic attacks sometimes occur. And the chances of a "bad trip" increase if a person takes Nexus when he or she isn't feeling well. People with psychiatric disorders, epileptic disorders, and blood circulation deficits also run a higher risk of having bad reactions to Nexus.

KETAMINE

Ketamine is a powerful sedative that is used by veterinarians as an anesthetic for cats and horses. An analog or chemical cousin of PCP, it has become one of the "club drugs." Because it has been used to incapacitate women, making them vulnerable to sexual attack, ketamine is also known as a "date-rape drug." As a result of its potential for abuse, the U.S. government classified ketamine as a controlled drug in 1999; its only legal use for humans is by prescription.

PATTERNS OF USE

Unlike many hallucinogenic drugs that are manufactured in clandestine laboratories, ketamine is usually produced legally and then diverted from legitimate sources such as veterinarians' offices and medical supply companies. On the street it is sold as a white powder or in a less-expensive liquid form that users mix with water or crystallize on top of the stove. Packaged in plastic bags or capsules and sometimes called "Special K" or simply "K," it is most commonly taken by snorting through the nostrils. Ketamine looks like cocaine and tastes a bit like methamphetamine.

EFFECTS OF KETAMINE

Like Ecstasy, ketamine has earned a reputation as an aphrodisiac. It is also reputed as useful in helping drug users come down from a cocaine or Ecstasy high. Ketamine can cause an out-of-body experience, giving the user the sensation that he or she has left his or her body behind and is viewing it from a distance. The initial effect from taking the drug is mildly euphoric, but repeated doses can bring about a sense of detachment from reality that may become psychotic. Blank stares and constricted pupils are typical effects from this drug. Many users have little desire to talk while under the influence of ketamine; others may speak gibberish.

Some ketamine users have spoken of a "K-hole," which refers to an unpleasant sensation that comes from using too much of the drug. An article by Alan Sverdlik in the *New York Post* quoted one user as saying the experience was "like being buried alive in a box and not knowing who you are, what you are, and why you are." Other users have found that they cannot move or speak while under the drug's influence. In fact, at high levels ketamine is fatal because it shuts down the respiratory system.

DMT

Dimethyltryptamine (DMT) is found naturally in a number of plants, especially some native to South America and the West Indies. It is one of the common ingredients in *hoasca,* the hallucinogenic beverage discussed in chapter 2. Closely related to psilocybin (also described in chapter 2), DMT has long been an ingredient in teas, some types of snuff, and other psychoactive substances used by indigenous peoples throughout South America and the West Indies.

Available as a synthetic substance today, DMT can be taken intravenously, drunk in a tea preparation, snorted, or smoked. Often marijuana is soaked in a DMT solution before the combination is smoked.

Typical dosages are 50 to 100 milligrams. DMT produces a fast and short-term hallucinogenic high. Effects usually appear within 10 minutes, and they disappear within an hour or so—a characteristic that has earned DMT the nicknames "businessman's trip" and "businessman's special." The experience is similar to that of an LSD trip, and some users consider DMT safer. However, anxiety attacks are much more common side effects with DMT than with LSD.

BELLADONNA ALKALOIDS

The plant known as belladonna (*Atropa belladonna*) grows wild in Europe, and it is cultivated in North America. It contains a number of alkaloids, including atropine and scopolamine, that have many medical uses. These alkaloids are used, for example, to dilate the eyes, relieve asthma, lessen motion sickness, and reduce cramps. The name *belladonna*, which in Italian means "beautiful lady," comes from its use by women, in earlier centuries, who would dilate their eyes to appear more beautiful.

At high doses, these alkaloids, especially scopolamine, have effects similar to those of hallucinogens. They bring on a delirium that resembles a weird dream. Frequently users feel as though they are flying.

Some modern users obtain *belladonna alkaloids* by prescription—or by prescription medications illegally diverted to the street. Another common source, however, is the jimsonweed plant (*Datura stramonium*), which contains some of the same alkaloids. The term *jimsonweed* is a corruption of the name Jamestown, the early colony in Virginia. Supposedly the first settlers, unaware of jimsonweed's effects, included its leaves in a salad. After eating, they became intoxicated and ill. Today's users of jimsonweed, seeking its dreamlike effects, generally boil the leaves to make a tea.

The typical side effects of belladonna alkaloids include a racing heart, dry mouth, increased temperature, and amnesia. At high doses these effects can be severe. In fact, at a high enough dose, the atropine alkaloid is lethal. As a result, the belladonna plant has earned the common name "deadly nightshade."

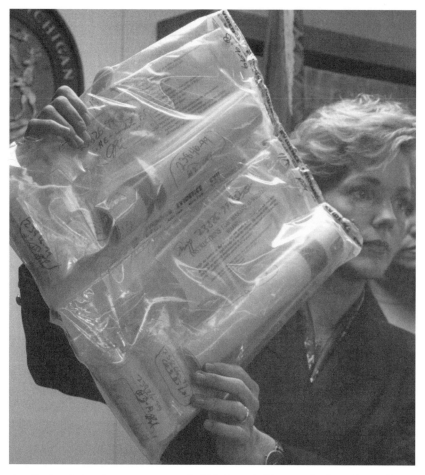

Jennifer Granholm, the attorney general of Michigan, holds up an "at-home" manufacturing kit for gamma hydroxybutyrate, or GHB, purchased by Michigan state police in an undercover operation. The hallucinogen GHB is a fast-acting sedative used as a date-rape drug.

OTHER HALLUCINOGENS AND RELATED DRUGS

Over recent years, various government publications, such as *Pulse Check*, have produced a virtual laundry list of other substances used either as hallucinogens or to control some of the effects of hallucinogens. Here are just a few:

- *Bufotenine,* a substance found in the skin glands of certain toads, has been used as a hallucinogen in experimental medicine and is sometimes taken by drug users. Some Native Americans traditionally milked the toad glands to get the drug. The high it produces lasts a very short time, and the side effects, which can include cramps and temporary paralysis, tend to be severe.

- *Gamma hydroxybutyrate* (GHB), sometimes known as "liquid ecstasy," is a rapidly acting sedative that is produced naturally in the body in small amounts. Synthesized in 1960, it was used by body builders in the 1980s because it appeared to assist in muscle building. Because of its euphoric and sedative effects, GHB was soon being used recreationally as well. Sometimes it is combined with hallucinogens to reduce or modify their effects. Like ketamine, GHB has also been used as a date-rape drug, and it has proved fatal under certain conditions. GHB is sold in vials or small bottles and is typically consumed by the capful or teaspoonful.

- *Rohypnol,* sometimes referred to as "roofies," is the trade name for flunitrazepam. Like GHB, it is used to enhance or cushion the effect of other illegal substances or to facilitate sexual assault. Elsewhere in the world it has been used by prescription, mainly for the short-term treatment of severe sleep disorders, but its manufacturer has never applied to sell it legally in the United States. Its adverse effects range from dizziness and amnesia to coma. Mixed with alcohol, the drug can be deadly.

It sometimes seems that users are willing to try almost anything that will alter their feelings and perceptions. Given the dangers, why do they take such chances? Although there is no definitive answer to this question, the next chapter considers some of the psychological and social factors that promote hallucinogen use and abuse.

Drug use begins for many reasons—depression, alienation, rebellion, a desire for new experiences, the need to fit in with a group. Because teenagers and young adults are particularly susceptible to these feelings, they may be in greater danger of succumbing to the lure of drugs than are their elders.

6

REASONS FOR HALLUCINOGEN USE

I n the heyday of psychedelic drug use in the late 1960s and early 1970s, therapist Dr. Robert Gould recorded the case of a 16-year-old LSD user named
Alice whom he had treated. Alice's family lived in the New Jersey suburbs
of New York. Though the family was prosperous and seemed happy, neither
parent was much involved with the children. After discovering that their father
was regularly cheating on their mother, Alice and her 18-year-old brother both
ran away from home. Their mother had known about the affairs but had
opted to tolerate them rather than seek a divorce.

Having dropped out of school, Alice joined a commune in the East Village
section of New York. The "baby" of the 10- or 11-member group, she was
cared for by the commune and not required to work. Sometimes Alice would
beg for food on the street "just for fun."

Gould found that Alice was quite depressed. She was using such drugs as
LSD and marijuana to escape from the pain and disillusionment she felt over
her family life. Alice's brother also got involved with drugs, eventually becoming a heroin addict. In Alice's case, Gould thought that drugs fulfilled some of
her needs for nurturance, trust, love, and security. The commune members
helped, too, by caring for her as they would a child.

As time passed, Alice would stay only in the immediate area of her new
home. Feeling safe in that environment, she refused to venture out of that
region for any reason. Gould concluded: "This girl was not psychotic, but for
all intents and purposes she was socially psychotic. She was so immature and
regressed, her dependency needs were so great, her frustration tolerance so
low that only drugs satisfied her needs quickly enough."

■   ■   ■

Alice's case illustrates how hallucinogen use—like the use of other drugs—
often connects to underlying personal and family issues. Drugs help the user

reduce immediate emotional pain, but at the same time they can prevent the person from dealing with the sources of the trouble. In this instance, Alice's drug use helped her ignore the deeper problems she had with her family. Instead of staying in school and ultimately becoming more independent from her family, both financially and emotionally, she fell into a pattern of drug abuse and prolonged dependence that turned a temporary trauma into a long-term struggle.

Hallucinogen use often begins in adolescence, when the tendency to feel insecure about oneself and unsure of one's ultimate identity is common. For young people such as Alice, experimentation with hallucinogens may appear to be one means of discovering who they are. Although there is no one single cause for hallucinogen use, we can look at some of the common psychological and social factors that lead people toward it:

1. *The need to escape from personal or family problems:* This was the most obvious factor in Alice's case. Because neither she nor her brother could handle the family situation, they both ran away from it—physically, by leaving home, and emotionally, by escaping into drugs.

2. *Rebellion against family or against society as a whole:* Often drug use is a way of rebelling against one's parents or of distancing oneself from the seemingly dull, conventional world of adults. Some people who take hallucinogens may feel they are making a statement, setting themselves apart.

3. *The desire to experiment, to discover new experiences:* Because psychedelic drugs have the reputation of opening the mind to new visions and startling insights, they may be attractive to young people who are bored with their own thoughts or eager to test their limits. LSD or Ecstasy may be seen as a quick route through what Aldous Huxley called the "doors of perception."

4. *The yearning for a new spirituality:* As chapter 2 illustrated, hallucinogens have long had a role in religious rituals in certain traditional societies. The counterculture of the 1960s and 1970s promoted the notion that LSD and its relatives could help the user reach a state of transcendence and undergo a deep religious experience.

5. *The desire to fit in with a group:* As with any other drug, peer pressure can be an incentive to participate in hallucinogen use. Peer

"Peer pressure" by means of ridicule or threats of exclusion from a group can influence young people to engage in negative behaviors, including experimentation with drugs.

The entertainment industry gets blamed for all sorts of social ills, from school violence to simple rudeness. In The Basketball Diaries, *Leonardo DiCaprio plays a high school basketball star caught in a world of drugs and violence on the streets of New York City. Although the movie was up-front about the consequences of addiction, drugs may seem more attractive on the screen than filmmakers intend.*

pressure doesn't necessarily mean outright urging from one's peers to take drugs. It can simply be the sense that a user fits in with the group and a nonuser does not. If a teenager's good friends regularly go to a club where they use Ecstasy, she or he may want to try the drug just to participate in their experience.

6. *Glamorization by the media:* Although there are plenty of anti-drug messages in today's mass media—on television, in magazines, on billboards—the media often glamorize drug use as well. The "heroin chic" of the 1990s was a good example; for several years some major clothing manufacturers hired models who had the underweight, exhausted look of heroin users. By promoting this

image as cool, critics felt, the ads encouraged heroin use. Similarly, during the late 1960s and early 1970s, advertisers capitalized on the hippie look, which may have helped to make hallucinogen use popular by association.

7. *The emphasis on immediate gratification:* We live in a high-speed age and are accustomed to rapid change and quick advances. Most people tend to feel rushed, short on time, and consequently short on patience. We want quick results. Some cultural observers believe that this attitude makes people more inclined to use drugs of all sorts. If they need to fall asleep, they take a sleeping pill; if they need to wake up, they take caffeine; if they need to escape the workaday world and renew themselves mentally and emotionally, they may take LSD.

There are many more factors that contribute to hallucinogen abuse. Virtually all of the problems of modern society, from the decline of the traditional family to the stresses of school and work, may be held partially to blame. For those involved with hallucinogen use, however, the main concern is how to get help. We turn to that question in the next chapter.

Overcoming drug abuse may require the discovery of its underlying causes. In individual therapy, patients confront their pain and learn to solve their problems.

7

GETTING HELP

D iscovering whether a friend or loved one has a problem with hallucino-gens—or with any other drug, including alcohol and marijuana—isn't always easy. Children as young as fourth graders sometimes begin experimenting with drugs. How can you know if friends are using LSD or PCP, and what should you do if you find out that they are?

HOW TO TELL WHETHER A FRIEND HAS A DRUG PROBLEM

It is not uncommon for people with drug problems to cover up their diffi-culties instead of seeking help. However, there are warning signs that can alert us to an individual's struggle with substance abuse. If you know someone who is exhibiting any of the following physical or behavioral changes, that person may need help:

Physical Changes

- *Dilated pupils:* having pupils that stay open much wider than usual

- *Dramatic change in weight or in eating habits:* having sudden signif-icant loss or gain in weight for no apparent reason; binge eating (*binge* refers to a pattern of excessive indulgence) or loss of appetite

- *Hyperactive behavior:* talking a great deal more than usual, demon-strating hyperactive behavior or the inability to focus on one thing

- *Loss of coordination:* stumbling, staggering, displaying shakiness, walking much more slowly than usual

- *Loss of memory:* showing a noticeable increase in forgetfulness

- *Marked change in sleeping habits:* sleeping a great deal or hardly sleeping at all; sleeping or waking at odd times

- *Tremors:* trembling or shaking of the limbs
- *Unusual heartbeat:* racing or irregular rhythm of the heart

Changes in Behavior

- *Absenteeism:* missing work or school frequently
- *Depression:* feeling frequently sad or blue, run down, or hopeless; having suicidal thoughts
- *Legal problems:* being arrested or getting in trouble with the law

A sudden change in sleeping habits, such as falling asleep at odd or inappropriate times, may be an indication that a friend is having a problem with drugs.

- *Poor school or work performance:* showing sudden decline in a student's grades or an employee's quality of work
- *Risk taking:* engaging in risky, dangerous behavior, such as driving when under the influence of some substance
- *Talking about drugs:* speaking frequently about drugs
- *Disengaging:* dropping out of sports, clubs, groups, and other activities; avoiding old friends

Many of these symptoms—such as depression, disengaging, and poor job or school performance—can, of course, have other causes. If you don't actually witness someone taking drugs, you cannot be sure of the reason for the person's behavior. Nevertheless, these danger signs often indicate that something significant is wrong. By contacting a guidance counselor, therapist, doctor, nurse, teacher, or other qualified adult, you can assist a friend in getting the help he or she may need.

SPECIFIC SIGNS OF HALLUCINOGEN ABUSE

Some of the symptoms of hallucinogen abuse resemble reactions to abuse of stimulants and amphetamines, sometimes called "speed" or "uppers." People under the influence of hallucinogens may speak too much or too quickly. They may pace back and forth or exhibit other forms of compulsive behavior such as repeating tasks over and over again or taking objects apart and then putting them back together. Often, too, hallucinogen users seem restless, nervous, anxious, or worried. Under the influence of PCP especially, they may react with unpredictable violence and aggression.

The mention of hallucinations, of course, is a key indicator that someone is using hallucinogens. The user may report having distorted perceptions of sight, hearing, smell, or touch. A fairly common complaint is of hearing a constant, imaginary buzzing sound in the background. After taking the drug, an individual may also suffer a severe headache or perspire a great deal. He or she may complain of having a dry mouth, and you may see that the pupils of the eye are enlarged. You may also see other characteristics listed in the examples of physical changes that are given in the first section of this chapter—such as trembling in the person's hands or fingers, the appearance of dizziness, or rapid breathing. An overdose of some drugs may cause convulsions and loss of consciousness.

Unpredictably violent and aggressive behavior can result from prolonged use of PCP.

Following binge use of hallucinogens, during which users often go without sleep for long periods of time, they may sleep for several days. If instead they remain awake as the hallucinogen wears off, they often feel ill. During this period, drug users can be a danger to themselves and to other people. They may become depressed enough to attempt suicide.

Another sign of hallucinogen abuse is that the users' overall health and hygiene frequently deteriorate. In addition to experiencing weight loss from failure to eat properly, they may begin to wash less often or neglect their hair, teeth, clothing, and general appearance.

In severe cases of long-term hallucinogen use, the user may develop psychotic symptoms. A person on hallucinogens may feel severely frightened and paranoid. As a result of hallucinogen psychosis, insignificant occurrences may cause him or her to become enraged.

WHERE TO SEEK HELP AND ADVICE

Every community has its own resources, such as emergency health clinics, community treatment services, hospitals, and health departments. You can contact school personnel, government officials, or health care professionals, and even check the phone book (or directory assistance) for help in treating drug abuse problems.

Numerous national organizations also offer hotlines, referrals, and treatment for hallucinogen abuse and related problems. See Appendix: For More Information for some places to contact.

EMERGENCY TREATMENT

Hallucinogen users who require emergency hospital treatment are frequently placed in a darkened, quiet room, where staff members provide reassurance and support and ensure that the patient doesn't injure him- or herself.

As discussed in chapter 4, doctors may administer medication to increase the rate at which the drug is eliminated from the body. For severe physical symptoms or psychotic episodes, physicians may administer medication to counter the effects of the hallucinogen. If the patient displays psychotic behavior, for example, the doctor may prescribe an antipsychotic drug such as Haldol (haloperidol).

If you are unable to persuade a hallucinogen user who is in distress to be taken to a hospital, you should make every effort to keep the person calm. Hallucinogen use can cause an individual to experience perceptual distortions that can make sounds seem very fast and high-pitched. Slowing your speech and lowering your voice may have a calming effect on the user. If you keep your movements slow and make sure your hands are visible, it may prevent the drug user from misinterpreting your actions as an attack. A PCP abuser who feels threatened may respond by attacking.

If possible, keep the drug user talking to help him or her stave off delusional thoughts that could lead to violent outbursts. For this reason, the person shouldn't be left alone. Try to encourage the individual to sit up or walk around since closed eyes often amplify the effects of the drug. Keep reassuring the drug user that the effects will wear off soon.

Remember, that the person's sense of time may be altered; a few minutes may seem like hours, and the individual's panic may increase. He or she may say, "It's been ages since I took the drug, and I'm not getting any better!" Explain gently that time distortions are also an effect of the drug and that they, too, will gradually wear off.

LONG-TERM TREATMENT

In the long term, when the patient has persistent anxiety or depression, a doctor may prescribe antianxiety or antidepressant medication. Because patients with a history of drug use may be inclined to adjust the amount of medication they take according to their own feelings or their own theories about their condition, the dosage must be carefully monitored.

Even with a cooperative patient, there is no magic medication that will prevent a hallucinogen user from abusing these drugs again. Therefore, most long-term treatment involves therapeutic counseling. As Marc Schuckit and Richard Schottenfeld explain in their contribution to the edited volume *Treatments of Psychiatric Disorders*, the therapist has three general goals in this treatment:

1. *Helping the patient achieve a life without drug abuse.* Even if the patient isn't a chronic drug user, the goal is almost always to help him or her stop using the drug entirely, not merely to reduce or moderate the use. This can be achieved in part by educating the patient about the drug's dangers and emphasizing personal responsibility. However, the patient often needs help in learning again how to live without drugs: how to deal with spare time, how to make friends who aren't drug users, how to reconnect with his or her family.

2. *Maximizing various aspects of the patient's functioning in daily life.* For therapy to be fully effective, the patient should be evaluated for any physical or psychological disorders that are independent of the drug use, and these should be addressed by the appropriate physicians. Often, too, therapists will help the patient deal with family or marital issues, job struggles, financial problems, even spiritual issues—anything that might send the patient into a tailspin.

3. *Preventing relapse into drug use.* To prevent relapse, therapists try to make patients vigilant about their own potential for slipping

back into drug use. Further, therapists help patients figure out what to do when confronted with a difficult situation. What if the former drug user accidentally finds him- or herself at a party where drugs are being handed out? If the patient has developed a plan for coping with that situation, relapse is less likely. Today's therapists also try to convey the idea that, even if the user weakens and takes the drug one more time, that is no excuse for continuing to take it—one slip isn't the end.

Hallucinogen users with severe troubles may need to be placed into a residential program, which may last three to five weeks. Residential programs provide inpatient treatment, which allows patients to escape from the surroundings that are part of their drug world, as they bond with peers, counselors, and staff. In most cases of hallucinogen use, however, therapy to help stop drug use takes place on an outpatient basis. The following sections review some of the therapeutic options.

INDIVIDUAL THERAPY

In individual therapy, the patient meets one-on-one with the therapist. The therapeutic techniques may include extended psychotherapy, in which the patient is led to examine deep-seated psychological conflicts and repressed emotions that may explain why he or she feels a need for drugs. Or the therapy may be more brief, homing in on the particular problems the patient faces and trying to develop effective ways of coping with them.

Much current therapy takes both a behavioral and a cognitive approach. That is, it focuses on helping the drug user discover new ways of acting and thinking that can head off the impulse to take drugs. This may mean learning to avoid situations in which drug use becomes more likely. Or it may mean learning how to direct one's thoughts in a different way at crucial moments.

FAMILY THERAPY

As Herbert D. Kleber and Marc Galanter point out in *Treatments of Psychiatric Disorders*, many doctors believe that the best therapy for substance-related disorders occurs in family or group settings. In family therapy, the therapist meets with not just the individual patient but also other family members—sometimes with the entire family at once.

For hallucinogen users who are adolescents still living with their parents, family therapy can be especially effective. The therapist helps the

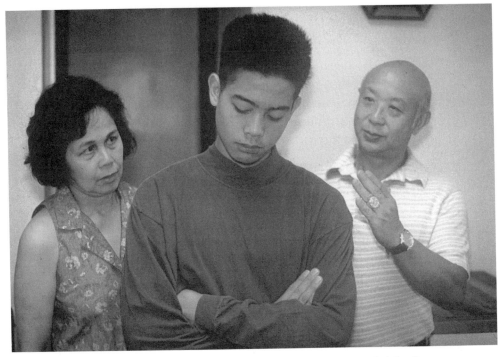

Because the toughest problems faced by young people often involve their families, many therapists believe that family counseling is the best solution for drug-related disorders.

family understand that the teenager's drug use is often the result of a pattern of family interactions. To change the result, the family can then work on changing the overall pattern. For instance, negative behaviors may be reinforcing one another: if the parents are overly critical, the young person may rebel by using drugs, which in turn will make the parents more critical. Therapists can assist in identifying such behavior patterns and working out methods for patients and their families to break away from them.

GROUP THERAPY

In typical group therapy, about 10 to 15 drug users meet jointly with a therapist, perhaps once or twice a week. This kind of session is probably the most common form of therapy for all kinds of drug abuse. A particular group may include individuals who have experimented with hallucinogens, marijuana, cocaine—any number of drugs.

The major advantage of group sessions is the support that patients receive from realizing they aren't alone—there are others with similar problems and worries. One patient's success story may encourage others. On the other hand, if one patient struggles, others can offer encouragement from the point of view of people who have "been there." The meetings can also help patients learn techniques of socializing with other people. The counselor in charge will guide the discussion, encourage participation, point out particular problem-solving techniques, and often teach some useful facts about drug abuse.

TWELVE-STEP PROGRAMS

Using Alcoholics Anonymous and its 12-step program as a model, many groups have developed similar programs for drug users. Narcotics Anonymous is one such organization with many local chapters. Self-help groups typically conduct meetings at which participants share their experiences and their concerns. A great deal of importance is placed on personal responsibility, but the members also try to assist and mentor one another. By adhering to the 12 steps, each member hopes to progress toward full and continued abstinence from drugs. There is usually a spiritual (though nondenominational) component to these programs.

The 12 steps of Alcoholics Anonymous, for example, require that alcoholics (1) admit their powerlessness over alcohol, (2) believe in the ability of a greater power to restore their sanity, (3) relinquish their will and lives to God, (4) engage in self-examination, (5) admit their wrongs to God, to themselves, and to one other person, (6) be prepared for God to eliminate their character flaws, (7) ask God to eliminate these flaws, (8) list and be prepared to make amends to all those they have harmed, (9) make amends to all those they have harmed if this is possible without injury to them or to others, (10) continue to engage in self-examination and admit when they are wrong, (11) pray for awareness of God's will and the ability to perform it, and (12) carry the 12-step message to other alcoholics and continue to live by its principles.

■   ■   ■

Some people go through therapy a number of times, in several different settings, before they recover completely. Nevertheless, the prospects for a hallucinogen user who willingly engages in therapy are good. Deep psychological or family troubles may not disappear as a result of therapy, but the patient can learn ways to handle his or her problems without resorting to drugs. Often, too, the therapy will help the former drug user become a stronger individual in all aspects of life.

APPENDIX

FOR MORE INFORMATION

American Council for Drug Education (ACDE)
164 West 74th Street
New York, NY 10023
(800) 488-DRUG
E-mail: acde@phoenixhouse.org
http://www.acde.org/

American Psychiatric Association (APA)
1400 K Street, NW
Washington, DC 20005
(202) 682-6000
http://www.psych.org/

Canadian Mental Health Association (CMHA)
2160 Yonge Street
3rd Floor
Toronto, Ontario M4S 2Z3
Canada
(416) 484-7750
http://www.cmha.ca/

National Clearinghouse for Alcohol and Drug Information (NCADI)
P.O. Box 2345
Rockville, MD 20847-2345
(800) 729-6686
http://www.health.org/

National Council on Alcoholism and Drug Dependence (NCADD)
12 West 21st Street
New York, NY 10010
(212) 206-6770
(800) 622-2255
http://www.ncadd.org/

National Institute of Mental Health (NIMH)
NIMH Public Inquiries
6001 Executive Boulevard
Room 8184 MSC 9663
Bethesda, MD 20892-9663
(301) 443-4513
E-mail: nimhinfo@nih.gov
http://www.nimh.nih.gov/

National Institute on Drug Abuse (NIDA)
6001 Executive Boulevard
Bethesda, MD 20892
(888) 644-6432
http://www.nida.nih.gov/

APPENDIX

U.S. DRUG SCHEDULES

Under the Controlled Substances Act, the U.S. government classifies drugs into five different schedules on the dual basis of medical usefulness and potential for abuse. Schedule I drugs bear the most restrictions on their use and distribution, Schedule V drugs the least.

Nearly all commonly abused hallucinogens have been placed in Schedules I through IV, as shown below. Most, in fact, are in Schedule I. For comparison, note that heroin, marijuana, and hashish are classified in Schedule I; cocaine, opium, and morphine are classified in Schedule II.

Schedule I

Criteria and restrictions:
- No currently accepted medical use
- High potential for abuse
- Research use only

Examples:

bufotenine	mescaline
DMT	Nexus
Ecstasy (MDMA)	peyote
LSD	psilocin
MDA	psilocybin

Schedule II

Criteria and restrictions:
- Currently accepted medical use
- High potential for abuse
- Available by written prescription only

Example: PCP

Schedule III

Criteria and restrictions:
- Currently accepted medical use
- Medium potential for abuse
- Available by written or oral prescription

Example: ketamine

Schedule IV
Criteria and restrictions:
- Currently accepted medical use
- Relatively low potential for abuse
- Available by written or oral prescription

Example: Rohypnol (flunitrazepam)

Schedule V
Criteria and restrictions:
- Currently accepted medical use
- Lowest potential for abuse
- Available over the counter

Example: preparations with limited amounts of codeine

Source: U.S. Drug Enforcement Administration.

APPENDIX

STATISTICS

The following statistics show some of the trends in hallucinogen use since 1992. "Lifetime prevalence" refers to the percentage of people who have used the drug at least once in their lives. A dash indicates that no statistics are available for the year in question. Figures for cocaine (which is not a hallucinogen) are included here for comparison.

Lifetime Prevalence for 8th Graders, by Year

	1992	1994	1996	1998
LSD	3.2%	3.7%	5.1%	4.1%
Ecstasy (MDMA)	—	—	3.4	2.7
Cocaine	2.9	3.6	4.5	4.6

Lifetime Prevalence for 12th Graders, by Year

	1992	1994	1996	1998
LSD	8.6%	10.5%	12.6%	12.6%
Ecstasy (MDMA)	—	—	6.1	5.8
PCP	2.4	2.8	4.0	3.9
Cocaine	6.1	5.9	7.1	9.3

Source: Monitoring the Future, "Trends in Lifetime Prevalence of Use of Various Drugs for 8th, 10th, and 12th Graders," Institute for Social Research, University of Michigan, Ann Arbor [on-line]. Available at http://www.isr.umich.edu/src/mtf/.

APPENDIX

BIBLIOGRAPHY

Aaronson, Bernard, and Humphry Osmond, eds. *Psychedelics: The Uses and Implications of Hallucinogenic Drugs.* New York: Doubleday, 1970.

American Psychiatric Association. *Diagnostic and Statistical Manual of Mental Disorders,* 4th ed. Washington, D.C.: American Psychiatric Association, 1994.

Blakeslee, Sandra. "Popular Drug May Damage Brain," *New York Times,* (15 August 1995): 5C.

Burtis, Carl A., and Edward R. Ashwood, eds. *Tietz Textbook of Clinical Chemistry,* 3d ed. Philadelphia: W. B. Saunders, 1999.

Concar, David. "After the Rave, the Ecstasy Hangover." *New Scientist* 154, no. 2087 (21 June 1997).

Creighton, F. L., D. L. Black, and C. E. Hyde. "'Ecstasy' Psychosis and Flashbacks," *British Journal of Psychiatry* 159 (November 1991): 713–15.

"Date Rape Drug May Have Caused Death of Girl, 15," *St. Louis Post Dispatch* (19 January 1999): A7.

Dupont, Robert, M.D. *The Selfish Brain: Learning from Addiction.* Washington, D.C.: American Psychiatric Press, 1997.

Executive Office of the President. *LSD: Facts and Figures.* Rockville, Md.: Drug Policy Information Clearinghouse, October 1998.

"Gamma Hydroxybutyrate (GHB)." ONDCP Drug Policy Information Clearinghouse Fact Sheet. National Criminal Justice Research Service, Rockville, Md., October 1998.

Goldstein, Avram. *Addiction: From Biology to Drug Policy.* New York: W. H. Freeman, 1994.

Gould, Robert. "Long-Term Psychological Management of Adolescent Drug Abuse." In *Management of Adolescent Drug Misuse: Clinical, Psychological and Legal Perspectives,* ed. James R. Gamage. Proceedings of the Second Annual Symposium of the Student Association for the Study of Hallucinogens. Beloit, Wis.: Stash Press, 1973.

Grob, Charles S., et al. "Human Psychopharmacology of Hoasca, a Plant Hallucinogen Used in Ritual Context in Brazil," *Journal of Nervous and Mental Disease* 184 (1996): 86–94.

Henderson, Leigh A. and William J. Glass, eds. *LSD: Still with Us After All These Years.* San Francisco: Lexington, 1994.

Hermle, L., et al. "Mescaline-Induced Psychopathological, Neuropsychological, and Neurometabolic Effects in Normal Subjects: Experimental Psychosis as a Tool for Psychiatric Research," *Biological Psychiatry* 32, no. 11 (1 December 1992): 976–91.

Hoch, Paul H., and Joseph Zubin, eds. *Psychopathology of Schizophrenia.* New York: Grune and Stratton, 1966.

Hoffer, A., and H. Osmond. *The Hallucinogens.* New York: Academic Press, 1967.

Hofmann, Albert. *LSD: My Problem Child.* New York: McGraw-Hill, 1980.

Hunt, Dana. *Rise of Hallucinogen Use.* Washington, D.C.: National Institute of Justice Research in Brief, October 1997.

Huxley, Aldous. *The Doors of Perception.* London: Chatto and Windus Ltd., 1954.

James, Jennifer. Psilocybin: *De-mystifying the "Magic Mushroom."* Tempe, Ariz.: Do It Now Foundation, 1999.

Jonnes, Jill. *Hep Cats, Narcs, and Pipe-Dreams: A History of America's Romance with Illegal Drugs.* New York: Scribner, 1996.

Keenan, E., M. Gervin, A. Dorman, and J. J. O'Connor. "Psychosis and Recreational Use of MDMA ('Ecstasy')," *Irish Journal of Psychological Medicine* (3 October 1993): 162–63.

Kleber, Herbert D., and Marc Galanter. "Section 4: Substance-Related Disorders: Introduction." In *Treatments of Psychiatric Disorders,* 2nd ed., ed. Glen O. Gabbard. Washington, D.C.: American Psychiatric Press, 1995.

Kuhn, Cynthia, Scott Swartzwelder, and Wilkie Wilson. *Buzzed: The Straight Facts About the Most Used and Abused Drugs from Alcohol to Ecstasy.* New York: Norton, 1998.

Langton, Phyllis. *The Social World of Drugs.* Minneapolis/St. Paul: West, 1996.

Lin, Geraline C., and Richard A. Glennon. *Hallucinogens: An Update.* National Institute on Drug Abuse Research Monograph. Rockville, Md.: U.S. Department of Health and Human Services, National Institutes of Health, 1994.

McGuire, Philip, and Tom Fahy. "Chronic Paranoid Psychosis after Misuse of MDMA ('Ecstasy')," *British Medical Journal* 302, no. 6778 (23 March 1991): 697.

Miller, J. D. *National Survey on Drug Abuse, Main Findings, 1982.* Rockville, Md.: National Institute on Drug Abuse, 1983.

Mitchell, I. J., A. J. Cooper, M. R. Griffiths, and D. J. Barber. "Phencyclidine and Corticosteroids Induce Apoptosis of a Subpopulation of Striatal Neurons: A Neural Substrate for Psychosis?" *Neuroscience* 84, no. 2 (May 1998): 489–501.

Monitoring the Future. "Long-Term Trends in Lifetime Prevalence of Various Types of Drugs for 12th Graders." Institute for Social Research, University of Michigan, Ann Arbor [on-line]. Available at http://www.isr. umich.edu/src/mtf/.

NIDA Infofax. "Ecstasy." "LSD." "PCP (Phencyclidine)." National Institute on Drug Abuse, National Institutes of Health, Rockville, Md. [on-line]. Updated March 1999. Available at http://www.nida.nih.gov/Infofax/.

Pollard, J. C. *Drugs and Phantasy: The Effects of LSD, Psilocybin and Sernyl on College Students.* New York: Little, Brown, 1965.

"Rohypnol." ONDCP Drug Policy Information Clearinghouse Fact Sheet. National Criminal Justice Research Service, Rockville, Md., June 1998.

Rosse, R. B., et al. "Phenomenologic Comparison of the Idiopathic Psychosis of Schizophrenia and Drug-Induced Cocaine and Phencyclidine Psychoses: A Retrospective Study," *Clinical Neuropharmacology* 17, no. 4 (August 1994): 359–69.

Rouse, Beatrice A., ed. *Statistics Source Book, 1998.* Washington, D.C.: Substance Abuse and Mental Health Services Administration, 1998.

Schazberg, Alan F., and Charles B. Nemeroff, eds. *The American Psychiatric Textbook of Psychopharmacology.* Washington, D.C.: American Psychiatric Press, 1995.

Schuckit, Marc A., and Richard S. Schottenfeld. "Overview of Treatment." Part of "Section 4: Substance-Related Disorders," in *Treatments of Psychiatric Disorders,* 2nd ed., ed. Glen O. Gabbard. Washington, D.C.: American Psychiatric Press, 1995.

Steinpresis, R. E. "The Behavioral and Neurochemical Effects of Phencyclidine in Humans and Animals: Some Implications for Modeling Psychosis," *Behavioral Brain Research* 74, nos. 1–2 (January 1996): 45–55.

Substance Abuse and Mental Health Services Administration (SAMHSA). "Tips for Teens: About Hallucinogens." Rockville, Md.: U.S. Department of Health and Human Services, 1998.

Sverdlik, Alan. "A Club Kid's Overdose Raises Fears about an Odd Drug of Choice," *New York Post* (27 January 1999): 16.

Ungerleider, J. Thomas, Robert N. Pechnick, Ann Bordwine Beeder, and Robert B. Millman. "The Hallucinogens and Cannabis." In *Treatments of Psychiatric Disorders,* 2nd ed., ed. Glen O. Gabbard. Washington, D.C.: American Psychiatric Press, 1995.

U.S. Drug Enforcement Administration. "DEA to Control 'Special K' for the First Time." Press Release. Washington, D.C., 13 July 1999.

U.S. Drug Enforcement Administration. "LSD in the United States." Drug Intelligence Report. Washington, D.C., October 1995.

U.S. Drug Enforcement Administration. "MDMA—Ecstasy." Drug Intelligence Brief. Washington, D.C., June 1999.

Vollenweider, F. X. "The Use of Psychotomimetics in Schizophrenia Research with Special Emphasis on the PCP/Ketamine Model Psychosis," *Sucht* (1992): 398–409.

Wodarz, N., and J. Boning. "'Ecstasy'-Induced Psychotic Depersonalization Syndrome," *Nervenartz* (July 1993): 478–80.

Wolfe, Tom. *The Electric Kool-Aid Acid Test.* New York: Farrar, Straus and Giroux, 1968.

Wright, H. H., E. A. Cole, S. R. Batey, and K. Hanna. "Phencyclidine-Induced Psychosis: Eight-Year Follow-Up of 10 Cases," *Southern Medical Journal* 81, no. 5 (May 1988): 565–67.

APPENDIX

FURTHER READING

American Psychiatric Association. *Diagnostic and Statistical Manual of Mental Disorders.* 4th ed. Washington, D.C.: American Psychiatric Press, 1994.

Carroll, Marilyn. *PCP: The Dangerous Angel.* Encyclopedia of Psychoactive Drugs. Philadelphia: Chelsea House, 1991.

Carter, Rosalynn, with Susan K. Golant. *Helping Someone with Mental Illness.* New York: Times Books, 1999.

Furst, Peter E. *Mushrooms: Psychedelic Fungi.* Encyclopedia of Psychoactive Drugs. Philadelphia: Chelsea House, 1992.

Henderson, Leigh A., and Glass, William J., eds. *LSD: Still with Us After All These Years.* San Francisco: Lexington, 1994.

Jonnes, Jill. *Hep Cats, Narcs, and Pipe-Dreams: A History of America's Romance with Illegal Drugs.* New York: Scribner, 1996.

Kuhn, Cynthia, Scott Swartzwelder, and Wilkie Wilson. *Buzzed: The Straight Facts About the Most Used and Abused Drugs from Alcohol to Ecstasy.* New York: Norton, 1998.

Trulson, Michael E. *LSD: Visions or Nightmares?* Encyclopedia of Psychoactive Drugs. Philadelphia: Chelsea House, 1992.

APPENDIX

GLOSSARY

Alkaloid: a type of nitrogen-containing compound found in many plants and some fungi. Many alkaloids function as drugs.

Belladonna alkaloids: alkaloids such as atropine and scopolamine that are found in the belladonna plant and in certain other plants, such as jimsonweed.

Catatonia: a complete lack of attention to surroundings, usually coupled with inappropriate stiffening or loosening of the muscles but sometimes also with excessive activity and excitement.

Delirium: an acute state of mental confusion or disorientation.

Delusion: a false belief that a person holds to regardless of external evidence.

DMT (dimethyltryptamine): a fast-acting, short-term hallucinogen found in many plants and also available in synthetic form.

Ecstasy (methylenedioxymethamphetamine, or MDMA): a synthetic drug that produces both psychedelic and stimulant effects.

Flashback: a recurrence of perceptual disturbances reminiscent of those experienced during an earlier hallucinogen intoxication.

Hallucination: a condition, usually involving sight, hearing, or smell, in which a person imagines that something is real when it isn't.

Illusion: a false perception or false interpretation of a real sensory image.

Ketamine: a powerful sedative drug and chemical cousin of PCP, often found at clubs and sometimes used as a date-rape drug.

LSD (lysergic acid diethylamide): the most potent known hallucinogen, synthesized from ergotamine tartrate, a substance derived from an ergot fungus that grows on rye and other grains.

MDA (methylenedioxyamphetamine): the parent drug of Ecstasy, with similar chemical structure and effects.

Mescaline: a hallucinogenic compound found naturally in peyote, a type of cactus that grows wild in Mexico and the American Southwest.

Neurotransmitters: chemical substances that transmit impulses between nerves.

Nexus (4-bromo-2,5-dimethoxyphenethylamine): a synthetic drug, also known as 2-CB, Erox, Bromo, and Spectrum, that is related to Ecstasy and mescaline.

Paranoia: a person's unfounded belief that he or she is being harassed or persecuted unfairly or is the victim of a plot or conspiracy.

PCP (phencyclidine): a synthetic, addictive drug, often sold illegally under the name "angel dust" or "crystal," that often causes sensory distortions, loss of coordination, amnesia, bizarre and aggressive behavior, and even short-term psychoses and long-term depression.

Psilocybin: a hallucinogen found in mushrooms of the *Psilocybe* genus.

Psychedelic: capable of changing mental functioning in ways that resemble certain psychotic symptoms, as hallucinogenic drugs can.

Psychosis: a severe mental disorder involving delusions or prominent hallucinations.

Schizophrenia: a psychosis that typically includes some combination of delusions, hallucinations, confused speech, and grossly disorganized or catatonic behavior.

APPENDIX

INDEX

APPENDIX

PICTURE CREDITS

page

8: © Science Source/Photo Researchers

10: © C. Robert Graham/FPG International LLC

12: © Prof. K. Seddon & Dr. T. Evans, Queen's University Belfast, Science Source/Photo Researchers

15: © Larry Mulvehill, Science Source/Photo Researchers

19: AP/Wide World Photos

20: AP/Wide World Photos

22: © Gary Retherford, Science Source/Photo Researchers

23: Francis Bacon, *Three Studies for George Dyer.* © ARS, N.Y. Private Collection, London, Great Britain. Giraudon/Art Resource, N.Y.

24: © George Post, Science Source/Photo Researchers

25: AP/Wide World Photos

28: Archive Photos

29: AP/Wide World Photos

31: AP/Wide World Photos

32: Reuters/Joe Traver/Archive Photos

37: © Science Source/Photo Researchers

39: © Larry Mulvehill, Science Source/Photo Researchers

40: © Ron Chapple/FPG International LLC

44: © Steve Horrell, Science Source/Photo Researchers

46: © Chris Michaels/FPG International LLC

48: © Barbara Peacock/FPG International LLC

50: © C. Seghers, Science Source/Photo Researchers

52: AP/Wide World Photos

56: © Tek Image/FPG International LLC

60: AP/Wide World Photos

62: © Ron Chapple/FPG International LLC

65: © Richard Hutchings, Science Source/Photo Researchers

66: Island Pictures/Archive Photos

68: © Dick Luria/FPG International LLC

70: © Michael Krasowitz/FPG International LLC

73: © Vcg/FPG International LLC

76: © Jeff Greenberg, Science Source/Photo Researchers

Senior Consulting Editor Carol C. Nadelson, M.D., is president and chief executive officer of the American Psychiatric Press, Inc., staff physician at Cambridge Hospital, and Clinical Professor of Psychiatry at Harvard Medical School. In addition to her work with the American Psychiatric Association, which she served as vice president in 1981–83 and president in 1985–86, Dr. Nadelson has been actively involved in other major psychiatric organizations, including the Group for the Advancement of Psychiatry, the American College of Psychiatrists, the Association for Academic Psychiatry, the American Association of Directors of Psychiatric Residency Training Programs, the American Psychosomatic Society, and the American College of Mental Health Administrators. In addition, she has been a consultant to the Psychiatric Education Branch of the National Institute of Mental Health and has served on the editorial boards of several journals. Doctor Nadelson has received many awards, including the Gold Medal Award for significant and ongoing contributions in the field of psychiatry, the Elizabeth Blackwell Award for contributions to the causes of women in medicine, and the Distinguished Service Award from the American College of Psychiatrists for outstanding achievements and leadership in the field of psychiatry.

Consulting Editor Claire E. Reinburg, M.A., is editorial director of the American Psychiatric Press, Inc., which publishes about 60 new books and six journals a year. She is a graduate of Georgetown University in Washington, D.C., where she earned bachelor of arts and master of arts degrees in English. She is a member of the Council of Biology Editors, the Women's National Book Association, the Society for Scholarly Publishing, and Washington Book Publishers.

Linda Bayer graduated from Boston University and earned a master's degree in English and a doctorate in humanities from Clark University. She worked with people suffering from substance abuse and other problems at a guidance center and in the Boston public school system. She was also a high school teacher before joining the faculties at several universities, including Wesleyan University, Hartford College for Women, American University, Boston University, and the U.S. Naval Academy. At the Hebrew University in Israel, she occupied the Sam and Ayala Zacks Chair. Bayer has also worked as a newspaper editor and syndicated columnist, winning a Simon Rockower Award for excellence in journalism. Her books include *The Gothic Imagination, The Blessing and the Curse* (a novel), several books on substance abuse, and five volumes for the ENCYCLO-PEDIA OF PSYCHOLOGICAL DISORDERS. Bayer is currently a senior speech writer and strategic analyst at the White House. She is the mother of two children, Lev and Ilana.